LIZ · LOCHHEAD

TARTUFFE

A · TRANSLATION · INTO · SCOTS
FROM · THE · ORIGINAL
BY · MOLIERE

D1421547

→ RENFREW

Third Eye Centre

POLYGON

POLYGON (D)

First published in Great Britain in 1985 jointly
by Polygon, 48 Pleasance, Edinburgh and
Third Eye Centre, 350 Sauchiehall Street, Glasgow

The publishers acknowledge subsidy from the Scottish Arts Council
towards the publication of this volume.

ISBN 0948275 17 0

Typeset by EUSPB, 48 Pleasance, Edinburgh.
Printed by E. Peterson, Laygate, South Shields.

C
2229
26.9.86

Introduction

I was approached by the Lyceum in the Spring of 1985 about the possibility of a brand new translation of Tartuffe for the company. I think I had probably once — mainly out of bravura and a heady ignorance of the difficulties — let it drop I'd love to try such a project some time!

Molière's Tartuffe is written in Alexandrines — iambic hexameters rhyming in couplets — but, conveniently convinced by a poet I met on a train that the hexameter was monotonous and alien to spoken English (not to speak of the Scots I was set on), I decided the really important part, the comic drive, came from the rhyming. So I set to, in rhyming couplets with a cavalier and rather idiosyncratic rhythm that I justified to myself by calling it "the rhythm of spoken Scots."

Actually it is a totally invented and, I hope, theatrical Scots, full of anachronisms, demotic speech from various eras and areas; it's proverbial, slangy, couthy, clichéd, catch-phrasey, and vulgar; it's based on Byron, Burns, Stanley Holloway, Ogden Nash and George Formby, as well as the sharp tongue of my granny; it's deliberately varied in register — most of the characters except Dorine are at least bilingual and consequently more or less "two faced."

There seemed to be a sensuous and sensual earthiness in Molière's masterpiece, a comedy *both* classical and black, and with an ending of quite explicit political satire which bland English translations totally lost. This is the way it came out — one killed-off character and all — when I tried to be faithful, in my fashion, to Molière's Tartuffe.

Liz Lochhead, 1986.

For Marion Keddie, Eleanor Aitken and the entire Lyceum Company with love and thanks.

Cast List

PERNELLE—**Anne Myatt**
ELMIRE—**Sarah Collier**
DORINE—**Juliet Cadzow**
MARIANE—**Gerda Stevenson**
CLEÁNTE—**Graham Valentine**
ORGON—**Stewart Preston**
VALÈRE—**Alan Cunningham**
TARTUFFE—**Andrew Dallmeyer**
LOYAL/OFFICER—**Billy McElhaney**

Designed by **Colin MacNeil**
Directed by **Colin MacNeil** and **Ian Wooldridge**
Commissioned by
The Royal Lyceum Theatre Co., Edinburgh
and first performed: **Friday, 24th January 1986.**

Opening

When the audience comes in *Flipote* and *Dorine* are in the lobby of *Orgon's* substantial townhouse. There are various doors off it, at least one ajar with a big slice of light cutting from it and occasional flurries of piano music, movement, and laughter spilling from offstage to where in the darkened (almost) hallway, our very bored maids smoke on the fly, do up each others hair into the back of their caps, peek into the offstage party, dare each other to drink some dregs on the removed sherry tray, play cards, yawn out over the audience etc.

Suddenly the hall light is snapped on with a blaze and *Pernelle*, who hasn't had much money of her own, but "likes a good thing" and has been well treated by her good boy business-man son, screams on, snapping at *Flipote* to help her into her good Copland & Lye winter coat, followed hotly by *Elmire* who is a beautiful, worldly, pragmatic (if not actually mercenary) young woman who, because her father is exactly of *Orgon's* class and origins is actually a whole generation more bourgeois, glossy and lazy than her husband. She is not unlikeable though, and her mother-in-law's kirkish moral superiority towards her puts us very much on her side (as she at least has some sense of humour). She is rather beautifully dressed, glossed and varnished in something, if at all, only a *little* Too Jewish . . . . Not *too* Bearsden-voiced either.

Then enter smirking *Marianne* & *Cléante* who from their different stances see it all. It is a mad dance, *Pernelle* turns first on one, then the other.

Act One: Scene One

PERNELLE: C'moan, Flipote, afore Ah get masel' inty a state.

ELMIRE: I can't keep up, you're going at such a rate!

PERNELLE: Wait, haud oan! I've had an ample sufficiency
Of your good manners, there's no necessity —

ELMIRE: Only nice to be nice, and, on the contrary
As my mother-in-law you're at least due civility.
But why so het-up, Mither, where's the hurry?

PERNELLE: Ah've to let this rammy a' go by me and no worry?
The wey you clan cairry oan is far from wyce.
There's nae respect. Ah try to gie advice,
But naw! There's that much argie-bargie it
's like nae place on earth but Paddy's Market.

DORINE: If —

PERNELLE: Can you no learn to shut your cheeky face?
You're jist a servin' lass, it's no your place
To stick your nose inty the business of your betters.

MARIANNE: But, Gran! —

PERNELLE: Wee Marianne. Obedient to the letter!
That auld-fashioned. So awfy-shy. Sae douce!
Butter widnae melt, she wouldny boo a goose.
Lukkin' oot thae big blue een and never blinkin' —
Ah bet your daddy's never shair whit you're thinkin'.

ELMIRE: But . . . Mither —

PERNELLE: Can you bring the wean up well
When you're scarce mair than a lassie yoursel'?
Her pair, deid, mither would turn in her grave
To see you spend, spend, spend what she scrimped to save.
A wummin needny get all dolled up sae fine
If it's only in her ain man's een she wants to shine.

CLÉANTE: Come, now —

PERNELLE: You're this bizzum's brother
Yet you and I have a lot of time for one another,
Am I right or am I wrang, eh, Mister Cléante?
You're . . . kinna half-sensible, yet I'd want —
If I were my son's wife — or him (which I'm no)
To ban you from this hearth, tell you to go.
How? Thae weys o' goin-oan, which you'd cry "mense".
Are mair leein' worldliness than honest commonsense.

3

CLÉANTE: Orgon's Mister Tartuffe is a paragon, no doubt —

PERNELLE: He is. See here, I take it ill-out
That you will scan him wi' that jaundiced eye!
Heed him. That man can not lie.

ELMIRE: If we only did what Tartuffe saw fit
It'd be a gey grey life with damn-all fun in it.

DORINE: Aye, hark at auld Narra-Mind and, afore lang,
We'd think ilka hermless thing we did was wrang.
Them that wants to can aye funn faut.

PERNELLE: My son kens Tartuffe is worth his saut!
He'd raither you were in God's Good Grace
Than daunerin' doon your ain paths tae the Other
                                                    Place.

MARIANNE: Neither dad nor anybody can convince me
That he's sincere. I tell you, since he —
From the word go I couldn't stick one thing about him.
Valère says wan of these days he'll clout him!

PERNELLE: And a' to sook in wi his future bride!
The big man! I'm shair Tartuffe is terrified!

DORINE: Ah cry it a dampt disgrace
That a naebody should tak' the maister's place!
To breenge in here, a raggity bare-fit tink,
Wi' the bareface to tell us whit to think.

PERNELLE: This humble hoose could be as a haly temple
If ye'd lukk-till his prayer, precept and example.

DORINE: You think wan thing, Ah think anither.
You cry him a saint, Ah cry him a blether.

PERNELLE: Oh the —

DORINE: Him and his flunkie, Ah'd show them
Ah didny trust them further than Ah could throw them.

PERNELLE: Aboot the sairvant, I neither care nor ken
But Tartuffe his maister is a Man Among Men
His truth's sairness and shairness is mair than you can
                                                    thole,
Yet his yin thocht is your immortal soul.

DORINE: Hell's bells, if a neebor draps by fur tea
Or Missis asks visitors in for a wee swaree,
Where's the herm? What does he think'll happen
That he nags us till our heids are nippin'?
What kinnuffa bawdy-hoose does he think this is?
Ah jalouse he's jealous of Missis.

4

PERNELLE: Haud yir wheesht, he's no the only yin
To be annoyed by a' the gauns-oot-and-in
And the caurs lined up wheel to wheel —
Some o' Elmire's cronies, they areny real!
Their sairvants are gallus, their gled-rags are garish —
She micht mean nae herm, but she's the talk o' the
pairrish.

CLÉANTE: Talk is cheap, and needs nae reason.
For gossip, ach, it's aye the silly season
And if we heed it, then we're dafter still.
We could not stop the idle tongues that wish us ill
Even if we shut our doors to our true friends.
Ignore it! Our self respect depends
On our clear consciences. Act fair and square,
And what folk say is neither here nor there.

DORINE: Don't tell me! It's Daphne next door
And that smouty wee man o' hers. They deplore
Loud and lang, their clarty-minds imagine
A'body but them's a bad yin.
Ah say . . . it's them wi' guilty secrets o' their ain
That are aye the first to cast the stane!
"Yon's a drunkert" "She's a hure!" Sich brattle!
It's a' a case o' the poat cryin' the kettle.

PERNELLE: Nuthin' to dae wi it! If you must know
It was Orante who tellt me so!
She's a guidly, godly soul and she
Has plenty to say about your company.

(THIS IS EXACTLY WHAT DORINE WANTS TO KNOW. HER
FACE REGISTERS SCORN)

DORINE: Well, nane can pick faut wi that guid wife!
Oh right enough she leads The Quiet Life —
At least since she got auld and past it!
She was wance so awfy-braw, but noo she's lost it
She's very passremarkable 'boot ither folk!
The vera idea o' a cuddle gies her the boke
Yet, wance upon a time, she had mair men up her
Stairs and up her skirts than she had hoat suppers.
There's nae airn sae hard but rust'll fret it.
There's nae cloth sae fine but moths'll eat it.
So it shouldny surprise us when a soor auld biddy
Turns her back on the world that's turnt its back on her
already.

(DURING NEXT SPEECH DORINE, ELMIRE & MARIANNE
ALL MIMIC PERNELLE BEHIND HER BACK AS SHE

5

WHEELS ROUND TO ALMOST BUT NOT QUITE CATCH
EACH OF THEM. CLÉANTE DOES NOT JOIN IN BUT
SHAKES HIS HEAD AND SMILES ON THE THREE WOMEN'S
COMPLICITY. PERNELLE CATCHES HIM SMILING AT THIS
& WRONGLY ACCUSES HIM OF MOCKING HER HALF WAY
THROUGH THIS NEXT SPEECH)

PERNELLE: (TO ELMIRE)
These havers are what you wish was true!
(TO DORINE)
I can't stand here all day listening to you
You neither ken nor care whit you're talking aboot
While yir fine mistress, day in, day oot
Mornin' noon and night wi a passion
Keeps this place gaun like a fair and fairs were gaun
                                          oot o' fashion!
But, if I can just get wan word in edgeweys tae mention
Somethin' that I fear you've yet to pey attention:
Till Tartuffe came you never knew that you were born
But my son never did yiz a better turn
Than to take inty his hame and heart this man
Who can convert you if anybody can.
He kens what's bad, he kens what's good and he
Kens what you should dae and what you shouldny.
Pairties and cerd-schools he canny abide
Because sich abominations are Auld Nick's pride.
And socials and swarrys and conversat-zionis
Will bring the wrath o' God doon oan us.
Oh, face to face it's kiss-me-luif and palsy-walsy
But ahint your back you should hear whit they all say!
It's: "That *will* be right" and "I kennt it!"
And "Yon yin's even blacker than he's pentit!"
Plenty reputations ruint, have nae doot!
Muck'll stick, when there's sae muckle fleein aboot.
And some folk are never happy till they're causin'
                                          trouble,
Yatterin' fit tae fill the vera tower o' Babel.
They'd frighten the French, and to cut a longstory —
Ach well, Cléante, Sir, so you funn me a bore, eh?
Snirkle away then, and smirk up yir sleeve,
Ah've had mair than enough, it's time to leave!
Be a while afore I set fit again in this habitation,
Which has taken quite a tummle in my estimation.

(HITS FLIPOTE)

Flipote! you're staunin' in a dwamm like a big daft dug!

6

PERNELLE: Get a move oan or Ah'll gie you a skelp on the lug,
cont. C'monty!
(EXIT PERNELLE, FLIPÔTE, MARIANNE)

Scene Two

(CLÉANTE & DORINE, AT EASE TOGETHER)

CLÉANTE: I'll jus stay here for now
In case, and for nothing, I get another row
From that old lady. She's beyond comprehension!

DORINE: You're no feart! You ken better than mention
The words "auld" and "lady" in the wan braith.
She'd say: you're nae chicken either, you're baith
The wrang side o' forty, but speakin' for hersel'
She thinks she wears her years extremely well!

CLÉANTE: No one said a word, she just hit the roof!
Incredible! She is quite besotted with Tartuffe.

DORINE: You should see her son, if you think she's fond!
He is daft aboot the schunner, it's beyond
Rhyme, it's beyond reason or any sense at a'.
Orgon. Yince a man sae full o' commonsense an a'.
In oor Troubles he picked the winnin' side, served Mr.
Prince
And loyally and bravely. — But his heid's full o' mince
Noo that he's under Tartuffe's spell —
He loves him Not Wisely but Too Well.
He whispers in his ear and cries him brither.
Loves him mair than wife, dochter *or* mither.
Ah'll never unnerstaun whit compels him
To listen to Tartuffe and dae whit he tells him.
Och, as much o' a mystery to get to the erse y
As whit yin man sees in wan wummin, or vice versy.
In fact he treats Tartuffe — noo Ah come to mention —
No unlike a lassie he wis winchin' . . . .
Oh, it's aye the Place of Honour, the tap o' the table for
The man who eats mair than ony other six were able
for.
It's, "Noo, here's a tasty pick, dinna let the plate pass
you."
And gin Tartuffe should rift it's, "My! God bless you."

(NOTE OF MOLIÈRE'S. A RARE ONE, SO IT MARKS HIS
OWN ASTONISHMENT AT HIS CHARACTER'S BOLDNESS
"IT IS A SERVANT WHO IS SPEAKING".)

DORINE: cont.	It makes me mad how everybody Can see my maister is enamoured o' a *cuddy*. Tartuffe canny brekk wind but it's a miracle. Or open his mooth but it's an oracle. Orgon bows doon to him in everything Lowps lik' a puppet when Tartuffe pu's the string Oh and peys through the nose for every sermon uttered Because yon yin weel-kens whit side his breid is

buttered

And hoo to herry money oot o' maister by a hunner

ploys.

Even his tyke o' a servin' man enjoys
The richt to harp and carp and criticise
Oor rouge and scent, which in *his* eyes —
Like lace and frills and a' thing the least fancy —
Are trappings o' devilishness and necromancy.
Nae sacrilege pit him in sic a tearing rage as
The hanky he funn in a hymnbook's pages!

Scene Three

(ENTER ELMIRE, THEN MARIANNE.)

ELMIRE:	Mither! She's said it all before once! Lucky you to miss the whole repeat performance. But here's my husband, I'm away before he sees me. Not one word, brother. Shsh! To please me. (EXIT ELMIRE)
CLÉANTE:	Suit yourself, sister. I'll stay If only to pass a civil time-of-day.
MARIANNE:	Uncle, darlin', sound Dad out about my wedding. He refuses to discuss it. I bet it's Tartuffe spreading Rumours and mischief. We're happy, that sticks in his

craw

So he's been gettin' at Dad to make him hum and haw . . .
Valère is mad about me and, needless to say,
I just can't wait to name the day.
And mibbe we —
(DORINE PRACTICALLY GAGS HER, JUMPS IN)

DORINE:	And here's the man himsel'.

Scene Four

(ENTER ORGON)

ORGON: (TO CLÉANTE)
Hello, hello, how's it gaun? You're lookin' well.

(MARIANNE'S SCURRYING EXIT, CLÉANTE ALMOST CONFUSED)

CLÉANTE: Its nice to see you. I'm just off.
How was the country? Green and stuff?

ORGON: Haud on brother — Since Ah've been away, Dorine,
Tell me, the last twa-three days, how's everybody
been?

(TO CLÉANTE)

See, yince hame Ah'm no' happy in masel'
Until Ah ken that a' the faimily's well.

DORINE: Day afore yesterday Missis took a bad turn, the worst
O' high fevers, a heid thumpin' fit tae burst.

ORGON: Och! An' Tartuffe?

DORINE: Tartuffe! Oh fine. I think
You'll funn him fitter than fower fiddles, in the pink!

ORGON: The sowell!

DORINE: Come dork, she wis richt weak
Wi' the gowpin' o' her sair heid and seeck
At the thocht o' touchin' a singel bite.

ORGON: Och! An' Tartuffe?

DORINE: Oh, he sat down with appetite,
Demolished a gigot o' mutton and a brace
O' pairtridge right religiously afore her face.

ORGON: The sowell!

DORINE: A' nicht she tossed and turned
And never got a wink, sae fierce her fever burned.

ORGON: Och! An' Tartuffe?

DORINE: Riftin', dozent and weel-fed
He left the empty dishes, socht his bed
Whaur he slept a' nicht unfashed wi' guilt
Fartin' ablow the feather quilt.

ORGON: The sowell!

9

DORINE:	It lukked serious, we talked her,
	Eventually, inty us sendin' fur the doctor.
	Her temperature was skyhigh he sat up till the crisis —
ORGON:	Och. And Tartuffe?
DORINE:	As large as life and twice as
	Ugly! In spite o' Missus' fainting fit, he recovered fine!
	And fortified himsel' wi fower jougs o' wine.
ORGON:	The sowell!
DORINE:	They're *baith* better, Oh, your every
	Concern, Ah'll tell Missus, wis for her recovery!

(EXIT DORINE)

Scene Five

CLÉANTE:	Brother! That bizzum's laughin' up her sleeve!
	And — excuse me butting in — but I believe
	She's got good reason. Why so blinkered?
	You were good enough to take him in, now the dirty
	tinker'd
	Take you to the cleaners! Charity by all means *but* —
ORGON:	You ken nothin' aboot nothin' so will you shut
	That mooth o' yours, brither, afore Ah get upset?
CLÉANTE:	True, I don't know the man personally, and yet —
	"By their *fruits* shall ye" — etcetera . . . .
ORGON:	Brother, brother if you could getra
	Chance to get to ken him, Ah ken you'd see —
	He's a man who's . . . a richt . . . *Man* and he —
	Och! To follow him is tae ken True Peace
	To feel this midden o' a world release
	Its haud upon ye. Chinjed man, that's me!
	Since Ah huv hud the benefit o' Tartuffe's company.
	He says wordly ties are so much vanity.
	And noo? Noo, wife, weans, mither could a' dee
	And it wouldny cause me *that* much pain!

(SNAPS FINGERS)

CLÉANTE: Oh that *is* nice, brother, real humane!

ORGON: Och, if only you'd have been there
             When Ah first encountert him and seen what Ah seen
                                                          there.
             He'd come each day to kirk wi' seemly modest mein,
             His hale soul's fervour shinin' from his een —
             Who wisnae inspired to see him kneelin' there,
             Lips gaun nineteen-tae-the-dozen in silent prayer?
             He Amen-ed and Hallelujah-ed and — the soul o' tact —
             Humbly begged me to receive this holy tract
             Which himsel' had funn sicc a boon and a blessing
             He was moved to Spread the Word in passing.
             Ah quizzed his servin'-man and he
             Haltingly confessed his Maister's poverty. (SHRUGS)
             Ah emptied my pockets, but, "For goodness sake it
             Is faur-faur too much" Tartuffe widnae take it!
             Ah insistit. Oh, he canny lukkeftir his sel' at a',
             Afore ma een, he gied the hauf o' it awa'!
             (Oh they must've seen him comin')
             Tae a' the cripples, cadgers and beggar-wummin!
             For his ain protection Ah brocht him hame wi' me
             Tae byde as yin o' the family.
             Och, he's Luck Aboot the Hoose, Tartuffe!
             Keeps a' thing richt ablow this roof.
             (LAUGHING)
             He watches my wife's good name, Ah must say,
             Ten-times mair jealously than Ah dae!
             Mind you, he's ower hard upon his sel',
             Yesterday the sowell wis right No Well,
             Fair scourged wi' guilt because, wi richt-good relish
             He'd cracked-deid a flea that bit him somethin' hellish!

CLÉANTE: Where's your reason gone, I'm shocked!

ORGON: Reason? Reason! God is not mocked!
             Freethinkers, eh? Is that what they cry you?
             I warn you: What's for you will not go by you.

CLÉANTE: This is the usual from your kind.
             You'd blindfold everybody else because you're blind.
             He who sees clearly what is to be seen
             Is a godless, freethinking libertine.
             Spare me the sermons, God is my witness
             And I'm not afraid to have him judge my moral fitness.
             Piety, like bravery can be put on, — if we're as silly's

11

CLÉANTE:
cont.
To believe in False Heroes and Holy Willies —
To fall for kidology and lose the place —
Not look for the true phizzog behind the falseface.
"The guinea-stamp is not the gold!"

ORGON:
Oh quite the philosoper! Well that's me told.
A solomon! A dominie! you're no' saft —
A peety that a' body but yirsel' is daft.

CLÉANTE:
Teacher nothing! Brother, I don't pretend
I'm clever — just, in the end,
It comes down to telling True from False.
Oh, nothing is more lovely than the quiet pulse
Of everyday piety in the true believer.
Nothing more sickening than the self deceiver —
The purveyor of platitudes that won't quite wash,
The sepulchre applying his own whitewash.
See, the ranting holyroller, born-again bigot, virgin
                                                    birther
Member of the Elect, latterday crusader, fundamentalist
                                                flat-earther,
Is often as sincere as he is round the bend!
Much worse, the blatant charlatan! For his own ends,
He cynically exploits what mankind most reveres,
Manipulates our deepest, most sacred, hopes and fears.
These days it's not at all uncommon
To hear fat, rich, priests decrying mammon.
Pastmasters all at twisting the text
So they profit in this world by way of the next.
They trade in pie-in-the-sky and (can you beat it?)
Here in this world they have their cake and eat it.
Doubly dangerous, these demons, whose best weapon
Is our reverence. We give them power to step on
Everyone and everything, and all in God's Name!
They are quick to anger, quicker still to blame.
They call down Heaven's Wrath to help them do their worst.
Before they stick in the knife and twist, they bless it first.
These days such villains are all around.
But altruism and true piety can still be found!
There are those who, quite without vanity,
Embody Faith and Hope and Charity.
You know such men. They don't show off
Yet their humane example is enough
To inspire us lesser men to emulate.
Arrogant preachiness is what they hate.
They are not always sniffing out intrigue; they find
Politicking absurd; they have no axe to grind.

12

CLÉANTE: cont.	They see the good in everyone and have the inner Strength to hate the sin, yet love the sinner. This is indeed the way to live! Frankly, your man Tartuffe, forgive Me, is not any kind of good example. You act in good faith, but the explanation's simple. A case of all that glitters and so on . . . .
ORGON:	Are you feenished, brother? Do go on!
CLÉANTE:	Enough said!
ORGON:	Thank God for that, excuse me . . . .
CLÉANTE:	One word! Let's change the subject, don't refuse me.
ORGON:	Uh-huh?
CLÉANTE:	A wee bird told me a certain young man By the name of Valère was to wed Marianne?
ORGON:	Uh-huh . . .
CLÉANTE:	And that you had fixed the happy day?
ORGON:	Uh-huh.
CLÉANTE:	Why than defer the ceremony?
ORGON:	Ah dinny ken.
CLÉANTE:	But you've had second thoughts, or third?
ORGON:	Mibbe.
CLÉANTE:	You mean then to go back upon your word?
ORGON:	Ah didny say that . . .
CLÉANTE:	Surely no just impediment To make a man break a promise he said he meant?
ORGON:	Mibbe aye, mibbe hooch-aye . . .
CLÉANTE:	Don't beat about The bush, what are you so suddenly discreet about? Actually, Valère himself asked me to ask you.
ORGON:	For heaven's sake!
CLÉANTE:	— A task you Are making very hard. What'll I tell the boy?
ORGON:	Whatever you like.
CLÉANTE:	Shall I say no joy? What are your plans, sir?

13

ORGON: I plan
          To let heaven guide me.

CLÉANTE: Come on man!
          You made Valère a promise then, it seems, forgot
          It. Will you keep your word or not?

ORGON: Tattibye!

CLÉANTE: Poor Valère! Altogether
          It looks like I better warn him. Stormy weather!

Act Two: Scene One

(ORGON ENTERS AND STARTS LOOKING IN CUPBOARDS.)

ORGON: Marianne!

MARIANNE: Daddy! (SHE ENTERS)

ORGON: C'mere to me
I want a quiet word.

MARIANNE: What are you looking for?

ORGON: To see
If anybody is hidin' tryin' to overhear.
This wee press is just the place for sicha nosy ear!
Naw, naw we're okey-dokey. Hmmm. Marianne,
                                   hen,
You're sicc an awfy nice-natured lass ye ken,
And you've aye kept yir auld daddy company . . .

MARIANNE: You've been the best daddy in the world to me.

ORGON: That's nice. If your wish to please me is heartfelt
You'll want to dae exactly whit you're tellt.

MARIANNE: To please ma daddy is to please masel'

ORGON: Hoo do ye feel about Tartuffe? Think well!

MARIANNE: Who me?

ORGON: Aye you. Take yir time, but Ah haveny
                               got a' day.

MARIANNE: Aw naw! Aw aye . . . Whit do you want me to say?

ORGON: Sensible question yon! Well, tell me, Marianne,
That our guest's a fine upstaunin' man,
You're awfy fond o' him, naebody ye'd raither
Mairry than Tartuffe, an' please yir faither,
Whit?

MARIANNE: Whit!

ORGON: Whit's up?

MARIANNE: Whit did ye say?

ORGON: Whit?

MARIANNE: Some mistake?

15

ORGON:	How?
MARIANNE:	*Who's* the man that I'm supposed to take? *Who* am I so awfy fond o' there's naebody I'd raither Marry? Shairly I didny hear you, faither?
ORGON:	Tartuffe.
MARIANNE:	But I do nothing of the kind, so why Would ma ain faither wish me to lie?
ORGON:	Because Ah want fur it to be true And whit Ah want should be enough for you.
MARIANNE:	Daddy, you widnae —

(DURING NEXT ORGON TIPTOES UP TO DOOR AND FLINGS IT OPEN)

ORGON:	Would Ah no! Tartuffe and you will mairry, so! That's that! A family alliance, got that clear? My mind's made up.

(DORINE, BENT OVER AT KEYHOLE, FALLS INTO ROOM)

Scene Two

ORGON:	Whit urr *you* daein' here? Nosy bitch to spy on us like that. D'you no hear 'bout curiosity an' the cat?
DORINE:	It must be just a kid-oan, shairly? Must huv the wrang end o' the stick, yet Ah'm fairly Positive Ah heard somethin' 'boot a marriage in the offin' That vernear had me die o' laughin'!
ORGON:	Is it sae unbelievable?
DORINE:	Oh aye, And Ah don't believe you don't know why!
ORGON:	Ah ken whit'll make you believe it.
DORINE:	Tell us a wee jackanory, we're a' ears to receive it!
ORGON:	Ah'll tell you, and soon you'll see it come to pass.
MARIANNE:	Oh naw!
ORGON:	Oh aye, nae kiddin' lass!
DORINE:	Och, didnae pey ony attention tae yir paw. It's jist a huntigowk!

16

ORGON:	Ah tell you — !
DORINE:	Nut at a', Naebody'll swally this!
ORGON:	Ah'm startin' tae get mad!
DORINE:	A'right, keep yir hair oan, but it's sad Hoo a man mair than auld enough tae be wise, Who sports grey hairs on whiskers o' sicc size, Could be daft enough to think he'd want —
ORGON:	The nerve! You tak' a lot mair liberties than you deserve To get away wi'. Shut yir face!
DORINE:	A'right, a'right, don't lose the place. Let's discuss this quietly and keep calm . . . Ah canny tell you how amazed Ah am. What would yon bigot want wi' oor wee lassie? He's plenty else to keep him busy! An who's he onywey, when he's at hame? How, wi' a' your money *and* your name You'd want a gaberlunzie son-in-law . . .?
ORGON:	Enough! We should lukk up to him who lukks doon on such stuff As getting and spendin', a' the world's gowd and gear. He's been ower concerned wi heaven to prosper here! Mibbe Ah cin restore his fortunes and fill his pantry — Back whaur he comes fae, ken, he's yin o' the gentry!
DORINE:	Gentry! Heard it, heard it! — Fair enough, unless The famous holiness disnae go wi' snobbishness? Och Ah see Ah vex you, but why sich swank? A'right! Stick to the man himsel', forget the rank. Think aboot it! To gie wee Marianne, Sae young and bonny, to sicc an auld man! Imagine the consequences it'd bring. Whit'd happen wid be the Usual Thing! To live the virtuous life is awfy chancy When a lassie's merrit tae a man she disnae fancy. And the man who kens the finger-o-scorn's Pinted at him because he weers the horns Has *made* his wife nae better than she should be! Pure? Merrit tae the richt man she could be . . . So the man who gie's his dochter's haun should ken that it's Him that's responsible for the sins she commits. Think! Afore you get her in sich slaister!

ORGON: Oh! The servin-lass gie's her orders tae the maister!

DORINE: Who could dae a lot worse than dae whit she'd tell him!

ORGON: Marianne! Don't listen tae this dampt haiverin' bellum.
          Trust your daddy, he kens whit's guid for ye!
          Ah ken, young Valère had made a bid for ye —
          But Ah've since heard he gambles, is a bit o' a drinker
          And, Ah suspeck, an atheistical free thinker —
          Ah don't see him at the kirk, he disnae go.

DORINE: Should he go at certain times and all for show?

ORGON: When Ah want your opinion, miss, Ah'll ask!
          Marianne, Tartuffe and his guidwife'll bask
          In Heaven's ilka blessing, and sich treasure
          Will merely crown their earthly pleasure!
          Like weans in the wid, like twa turtledoos
          Like a richt perra lovebirds, like coos
          Rolling in clover, like moths tae the light
          They'll attract yin anither, happy as pigs in — right
          Piggy-paradise, that's the pure and simple y it!
          An' — a clever lass can aye mak' a man tae fit her
                                                      template.

DORINE: She canny mak' a silk purse oot a soo's erse!

ORGON: The language!

DORINE: An eejit is an eejit, nothin' worse!
          Yon yin husnae got the sense he wis born wi!
          Plenty bumps on his heid, but, tae grow horn wi!

ORGON: Dinna interrupt! Cin you no learn
          No tae stick yir nose inty whit's nane o' yir concern?

          (TURNS TO SPEAK TO MARIANNE, BUT EACH TIME
          DORINE INTERRUPTS HIM AS SOON AS HE GOES TO OPEN
          HIS MOUTH)

DORINE: Ah wid say nuthin' if Ah didny care aboot ye!

ORGON: That's awfy guid o' ye. Ah could dae withoot ye . . .

DORINE: And 'cos Ah care —

ORGON: Who cares if you care or no!

DORINE: But Ah'll care 'boot you onywey, Ah will so!

ORGON: Ocht! Will you shut up?

DORINE: Ah cry it a sin
          Yon's the sort o' alliance ye want yir dochter in.

ORGON: You brassnecked neb you, ya bletheranskite —

DORINE:	Whit! Is this the big religious man, dae Ah hear right?
ORGON:	A saint'd lose patience, you should be hung! For the last time, Ah mean it! Haud yir tongue.
DORINE:	If Ah don't speak oot, Ah'll think it a' the mair.
ORGON:	Think whit you like, but open yir mooth, beware! (TO MARIANNE) Ah've thocht o' everythin' —
DORINE:	(ASIDE) Ah'm fair beelin' At no bein' able to say whit Ah'm feelin'. (BUT AS ORGON TURNS TO HER SHE ALWAYS SHUTS UP. HE ALWAYS TURNS BACK THEN TO MARIANNE.)
ORGON:	Tartuffe isny o' yir dandified or cissy ilk And yet his face is . . .
DORINE:	Fit tae turn the milk!
ORGON:	. . . Is such that, even if you don't care For his other qualities —
DORINE:	Och aye, A Lovely Pair! If Ah wiz her, nae man'd mairry me, No if Ah didny want him! He'd soon see, And see afore the weddin' day was by, Ye can tak' a wife tae bed but ye canny mak' her lie.
ORGON:	You mean tae tak' nae heed o' whit Ah say?
DORINE:	Whit's up? It isny you Ah'm talkin' tae.
ORGON:	Who were ye talkin' tae, then?
DORINE:	Masel'.
ORGON:	A' richt. Naebody cin say Ah didny warn her well! (HE PREPARES TO SLAP DORINE'S FACE BUT SHE'S STANDING MUM & MUTE EVERY TIME HE LOOKS AT HER) Ah'm forced to gie her the back o' ma haun . . . (TO MARIANNE, TEMPTING & DARING DORINE) Ah ken ye'll be happy, learn tae unnerstaun — The man Ah've picked — The future Ah've mapped oot so well. (BURSTS) How are you no talkin' tae yirsel?
DORINE:	Ah've naethin' tae say.
ORGON:	Jist wan word —
DORINE:	Ah talk when it suits me.
ORGON:	Cheep awa', wee burd!
DORINE:	Ah'm no sae daft.

ORGON:	A'richt, Marianne, You've tae dae everythin' Ah tell ye an' mairry this man.
DORINE:	(BURSTS OUT THEN RUNS AWAY, DODGING BLOW) *Ah'd* be daft enough tae mairry him an' Ah don't think!
	(HE TAKES A SWIPE, BUT MISSES OF COURSE)
ORGON:	That maid o' yours wad drive me tae drink. Ah'm no fit to continue the conversation thanks to yon. Ma bloodpressure's up an ma insides are gaun! Ah better funn ma medicine an' dose masel'. Tak' a turn aboot the gairden an' compose masel'.
	(EXIT ORGON LEAVING MARIANNE & DORINE)

Scene Three

DORINE:	Huz the cat got your tongue, or whit? Leavin' me tae say your bit! The hale thing's ridic-ulous, nae sense t'it But naw, ye nivir said a word against it.
MARIANNE:	Ma faither's the Big Boss, let's drop it —
DORINE:	Say onythin', dae onythin', but *stop* it.
MARIANNE:	Say what?
DORINE:	Tell him ye canny boss the hert aboot. Say love is the wan thing ye'll no mairry withoot. Say if he's so ta'en oan wi Tartuffe, oh well Mibbe he should mairry him himsel'.
MARIANNE:	His power over me's as absolute as it's absurd! And I'm feart tae say a single word.
DORINE:	C'moan! Valère's already asked ye, so Tell me, d'you love him, eh, or d'you no?
MARIANNE:	Oh Dorine, that isny fair! How can you ask! You know how much I care. Day and night you've been my confidante You know Valère's the only man I'll ever want.
DORINE:	How dae Ah ken a' that heart-tae-heart Wisnae jist talk, and playin' the part?
MARIANNE:	Dorine, I can't tell you how hurt I feel If even you can doubt my love is real.

20

DORINE:	Then you love him?
MARIANNE:	More than my life.
DORINE:	And he loves you?
MARIANNE:	Enough to make his wife.
DORINE:	Fine. And how aboot the big Tartuffe Marriage Plan.?
MARIANNE:	I'll kill myself before I'm forced to marry such a man.
DORINE:	Oh very good! Ah must be daft to no see The easy wey oot o' a' this hertbrek is tae dee! Is yon no awfy sensible, the very dab! My! self peety fair gies ye the gift o' the gab.
MARIANNE:	You're that crabbit, you're no offering Much help or pity for me in my suffering.
DORINE:	Nae peety for them that cause a big stramash and yit Jist gie in when it comes tae the bit.
MARIANNE:	I'm feart to just say I'll no wed him!
DORINE:	Love asks you hae a lover's smeddum!
MARIANNE:	It's no a question of how much I love Valère. He should deal wi dad for me, so there!
DORINE:	Guid kens yir da's deleerit ower yon! But whit Valère's done wrang, Ah fail tae unnerstaun. Because he took Orgon at his word but noo discovers Yir dad's gone back on it, the faut's your lovers?
MARIANNE:	Am I supposed to be stubborn and defiant Pit my wee self against my dad, the giant? Is it no kinna unfeminine to flaunt Before the whole wide world how much I want Valère? Should a lassie disobey her faither?
DORINE:	Of course she shouldny, no when she'd raither Have yit another auld man to belang tae! Tartuffe! That's grand! 'Deed Ah'd be wrang tae Try and pit yi aff, faur be it fae me! Jined wi Mister Tartuffe in Holy Matrimony! That's no tae be sniffed at, he's — so the world's heard — The Big Aristocrat — in his ain back-yerd. Wi' his rid, plooky grunzie — is he no quite it! If you're pleased hen, I'm delightit.
MARIANNE:	Aw naw!
DORINE:	Oh aye, ye'll be mistress o' sich cherms When ye lie a' nicht in yir bridegroom's erms . . .

21

MARIANNE: Don't! Ah canny. Tell me whit tae dae.

DORINE: Naw naw, A biddable good-lassie must obey
Her faither if he'd wad her tae a puggy-ape!
Yir future's rosy, dinna ettle tae escape.
He'll tak' ye till his ain neck o' the wids
Introduce ye tae his clan o' cousins, bluid's
Thicker than watter, they'll be yir sole society.
— Bar the cooncillor's wife who, wi' propriety
Will tak' you ben the parlour, dust the chair
Afore she says "Noo park your erse doon there".
Mibbe yince a year there'll be a galaday
Wi' twa sets o' bagpipes an' a flag fur the holiday!
And if your man —

MARIANNE: Over my dead body, Dorine!
Tell me how to get out of it, don't be mean.

DORINE: Ah'm jist the servant —

MARIANNE: Oh in the name!

DORINE: Yi deserve tae go through wi' it a' the same.

MARIANNE: Dorine, pet!

DORINE: Naw.

MARIANNE: I swear to you, I'll die!

DORINE: Naw, Tartuffe's the bed yiv made, and ye maun lie.

MARIANNE: Help me, I've always trusted you, I've aye relied —

DORINE: Naw, it serves ye richt if yir Tartuffified!

MARIANNE: Very well. I suffer. You don't care
So leave me now, alone with my despair. —
Despair which shall teach my misery
The One, Unfailing, Final Remedy . . .

(TURNS TO GO, DORINE STOPS HER)

DORINE: Haud oan, it seems yi need Auld Dorine's help at last
In spite o' a' yir dampt cheek in the past?

MARIANNE: Abandon me to this Living Hell, you
Abandon me to Death. I'll die, I tell you!

DORINE: There, there, we'll fox them, be ower clever
For the likes o' them. Well, here's the lover!

22

Scene Four

(ENTER VALÈRE)

VALÈRE: Aha! Exactly who I'd choose to see —
I just heard some news that certainly was news to me.

MARIANNE: What?

VALÈRE: That you are marrying Tartuffe.

MARIANNE: It's true
My father seems to have this end in view.

VALÈRE: Your father, miss, —

MARIANNE: Decided I'm at his disposal
Reversed our plans and made a new proposal.

VALÈRE: What! In seriousness?

MARIANNE: In seriousness
He tells me my only answer can be yes.

VALÈRE: And did you tell him where to go?

MARIANNE: What do you think I told him?

VALÈRE: I don't know!

MARIANNE: Well if you don't know, I don't either!

VALÈRE: You don't?

MARIANNE: I don't.

VALÈRE: That's honest! Suppose it's neither
Here nor there as far as I'm concerned . . .

MARIANNE: It's what?

VALÈRE: No skin off my nose quite honestly, it's not!

MARIANNE: It's not?

VALÈRE: Not really . . .

MARIANNE: No? That's nice.
All the same I'd be awfully glad of your advice.
Should I marry him or not?

VALÈRE: Of course!
Marry the man, you could certainly do worse.

MARIANNE: You're right, I'll do it! Thanks for the Balanced View.

VALÈRE: Evidently this prospect is agreeable to you.

MARIANNE: As agreeable as your of role of Agony Aunt?

23

DORINE:	(ASIDE)
	A quarrel is a hellish whirlpool lovers *want*.
	They must! They *will* wade in an' hit oot blindly.
MARIANNE:	(TO VALÈRE)
	Thank you for your counsel, I know you meant it kindly.
VALÈRE:	A pleasure, madam, to give you the answer you desired.
MARIANNE:	You wish me to marry him, sir, I'll do what's required.
DORINE:	(TO HERSELF)
	Leave them, Dorine, tae their fechts and fankles . . .
	(WITHDRAWS & LOOKS ON WITH AMUSEMENT)
VALÈRE:	You never loved me, that's what rankles.
	Boy! When I think how easily I was deceived!
MARIANNE:	Huh! And the advice that I received!
	Don't talk to me of "never loved", excuse me!
	I'll marry who you advised me to, since you refuse me.
VALÈRE:	Advice nothing! Excuse enough
	To spurn my love and break it off.
MARIANNE:	That will be right!
VALÈRE:	Of course it is
	You're over the moon you're going to be his.
MARIANNE:	Think what you want to think, I don't mind.
VALÈRE:	I will. And mibbe I'll pay you back in kind.
	I know another lady and I'm Well In there . . .
MARIANNE:	Sure, not a female in the world but fancies Valère!
VALÈRE:	Obviously not true, since *you* don't.
	But *someone* might, if you won't.
	I'm sure some sweet, kind lady can be found
	To dish out consolation on the rebound!
MARIANNE:	The gap I leave is not so big you won't fill it.
	Be real easy to find someone better, will it?
VALÈRE:	I'll do my best. Hell, it's self-defence!
	Losing you has wrecked my confidence.
	But, if the wounds of love are far from healed,
	Still, in like Flynn and play the field,
	Lay on Macduff — rather than be humiliated
	Being seen to love where it's not appreciated.
MARIANNE:	How noble! How too, too masculine!

VALÈRE:	*Anyone* following these principles is doing fine. I've to keep my flame of love for you a white hot anguish? You'd want me to be lovelorn? I've to languish While visions of you and him dance in my head And not put my love elsewhere instead?
MARIANNE:	On the contrary, find some slut then! Do your stuff. Far as I'm concerned yesterday's not soon enough.
VALÈRE:	I'm sure you're happy all this has resulted In my leaving you for ever, totally insulted?
	(HE GOES TO LEAVE, BUT KEEPS RETURNING, AGAIN & AGAIN)
MARIANNE:	Too true!
VALÈRE:	I want you to remember thanks to you, alas, Matters between us have come to total impasse.
MARIANNE:	Uh-huh!
VALÈRE:	My plan is very simple. You marry? I'll follow your example.
MARIANNE:	So be it.
VALÈRE:	So be it indeed, okey-dokey, right-oh!
MARIANNE:	Fine!
VALÈRE:	Last time you'll see me, I want you to know.
MARIANNE:	I'll survive.
VALÈRE:	Eh?
MARIANNE:	Eh what?
VALÈRE:	Did you shout?
MARIANNE:	Me, you're dreaming!
VALÈRE:	I'm on my way out You hear me? Goodbye!
MARIANNE:	Goodbye, good riddance!
DORINE:	Hoi, Ah nivir heard sich bliddy nonsense. You're a daft pair o' articles, ah don't know! Ah let ye fight, tae see hoo faur ye'd go. Hoi! Stoap Valère.
VALÈRE:	What's up, Dorine?
DORINE:	C'mere!
VALÈRE:	No, I'm adamant, I mean To leave once and for all, at *her* suggestion!

25

DORINE:	Stoap!
VALÈRE:	I can't. It's quite out of the question.
MARIANNE:	Evidently he can't stand to see my face! *I'll* go and leave him plenty empty space.

(MARIANNE GOES TO LEAVE. DORINE LETS GO OF VALÈRE AND GRABS HER)

DORINE:	Another yin! Where ye gaun?
MARIANNE:	Leave me!
DORINE:	Haud oan!
MARIANNE:	No! No, Dorine I'm off, leave me alone.
VALÈRE:	*I'll* be the one to go, I feel compelled. Marianne looks at me as though I smelled.

(DORINE GRABS HIM STILL HANGING ON TO MARIANNE)

DORINE:	Again! Yiz'll be the daith o' me! Don't be stupit! C'mere the baith o' ye.
MARIANNE:	Dorine, what do you want with us?
VALÈRE:	I fear we've nothing further to discuss.
DORINE:	Ah'm gonny sort this fankle oot, cause some'dy needs Tae! Are ye baith aff yir heids?
VALÈRE:	She said a lot of things I can't forget.
DORINE:	Urr ye an eejit or urr ye an eejit tae get upset?
MARIANNE:	I was treated in a very pretty fashion!
DORINE:	Daft as each other! Her yin passion Is you and yours, I swear! And this boay couldny love you mair. He's fairly burnin' tae be yir man. C'moan Valère! Acht! Marianne . . .
MARIANNE:	Why then give me such advice?
VALÈRE:	Why ask me? That wasn't very nice.
DORINE:	A perra loonies! Gie's yir haun's, you twa. (TO VALÈRE) Yours first!
VALÈRE:	What for?
DORINE:	(TAKING MARIANNE'S & LINKING THEM) Yours an' a'!
MARIANNE:	What exactly is the point of this?

26

DORINE:	Guid's sake, gi'e yin anither a Wee Kiss. Sic a remedy wid be entirely . . . efficacious.
VALÈRE:	(TO MARIANNE) Give me a civil look then, don't be ungracious!
DORINE:	De'il kens, but lovers are gey thrawn craturs . . .
VALÈRE:	No wonder men end up as women-haters. After all those cruel, cruel things you've spoken — It's not just Valère's poor *heart* you've broken!
MARIANNE:	You're a most ungrateful man! That's great!
DORINE:	Enough o' a' this argie-bargie and debate — Hoo can we pit a stoap tae this accursit mairrage?
MARIANNE:	Let's stop it, please! Valère, screw your courage! (ONCE HE'S WORKED OUT THIS ISN'T AN INSULT HE GRABS HER AND THEY KISS. THEY KISS AND STOP AND KISS AGAIN ALL THROUGH DORINE'S NEXT (PRACTICAL) SPEECH SO SHE'S CONSTANTLY EXASPERATED THAT THEY'RE TAKING NOTHING IN)
DORINE:	If yir dad's conscience disnae prick him, Then, somehow, we'll funn a wey to swick him. Let oan yir fu' fae tap to toe wi' dochterly devotion An' that ye 'gree till the hale jingbang o' a notion. Then, when it comes tae the bit, the weddin' Can aye be pit aff at a fiddler's biddin'. Yin time, yir no weel — a sair heid, or worse; Anither ye broke a mirror; or met a hearse As ye were on yer wey tae kirk; you're in a guddle Ower a bad dream 'boot mucky watter in a puddle Or . . . ye seen a single pyat, a burd o' sicc ill omen The day's nae day tae mak' ye a mairrit wummin. An' here's yir trump-cerd, unless ye say "I do", Nae man oan earth can be yokit tae you. Hooever, in oarder tae best speed our thrivance, You two ignore each other, that's oor furst contrivance! (OF COURSE RIGHT NOW THEY ARE ANYTHING BUT IGNORING EACH OTHER. DORINE PRISES THEM APART, AND TO VALÈRE)
DORINE:	Get tae! Enlist yir freens in a campaign To mak' her faither gie whit's, eftir a', yir ain! As for us, we've a'ready the stepmither On oor side, next: that Man o' Pairts, her brither.
VALÈRE:	Whatever is the end of all our machinations In you, my darling, lie my dearest aspirations.
MARIANNE:	If my cruel father should insist on tearing us apart Still no man but Valère shall ever rule my heart.

DORINE: Would lovers no deive you, their mooth's don't stap!
I said, get tae!

VALÈRE: Another thing —

DORINE: Yap, yap, yap!
Yir tongue's gaun like the clappers, ye blether.
You go wan wey — and *you* go the ither!

(SEPARATES THEM & SHOVES THEM OFF, ONE EACH SIDE,
STANDS ARMS AKIMBO, BREATHING.)

Act Three: Scene One

(DORINE'S RESPITE SHATTERED AS FIRST VALÈRE, THEN A
MOMENT LATER MARIANNE, FROM THEIR RESPECTIVE SIDES
REAPPEAR.)

VALÈRE: May God strike me dead — No don't call me rash,
I mean it. Tartuffe! I'll settle his hash,
I'll — I don't deserve to be called a man
If any power in the world keep me from Marianne.

(THE LOVERS RUSH INTO EACH OTHERS ARMS.)

.DORINE: Oh aye, "Haud ma jaicket!" — Haud yir hoarses,
Orgon mibbe isny serious, of course he's
Likely no! Onywey, fechtin', whaur's the sense in that?
A loat mair weys than yin tae skin a cat . . .

MARIANNE: Oh don't do it Valère! D'you think I'd enjoy to see
Two grown men fighting, and all over me?
Forget Tartuffe! I'd never marry him anyway.
Dorine'll tell you I refused point blank. No way!

DORINE: But yir stepmither! Gently does it baith o' ye —
She'll soart Tartuffe, and yir faither tae!
Tartuffe's aye sookin' in wi her and it's ma theory
He's got an awfy soft spot fur Elmire. Eh?
You've never noticed? Mibbe Ah read too much intae
The slaiverin' pee-hereness that you're blin' tae . . .
At ony rate: Missis somehow discovered
Orgon's daft scheme and how yir lover'd
Jist get the bum's rush, wi' nae by-yir-leave,
So ye'd mairry Tartuffe — well she couldnae believe
It! How could it come up Orgon's humph
To abandon his dochter tae yon big sumph?
As for yir wee pow-wow, she wis jist remarkin'
How she'd gie her eye-teeth t' be able tae hearken
(Flee-on-the-wa' style) tae you an' yir pop . . .
Ah says, "Ah'll funn a hidey-hole . . ." She goes, "Eavesdrop?"
Ah goes "Aye", she goes, "Naw! I couldny encourage it."
Ah goes, "Suit yirsel', well!" She says, "Could you
manage it?"
Well: nothin' fur it, tae cut a longstory shoart,
But fur me tae hide, hearken and report —
Back tae Elmire, like — whether it was true.
So! Ah've an eye tae the keyhole keekin' through
Takin' a' thing in, when whit should happen
But Orgon catches us! Rid-haundit, ears flappin',

DORINE: cont.	Nae maitter! Afore a' this, Elmire Asked me tae ask Tartuffe tae meet her here, Aye, *she'll* sound him oot aboot this merridge — She's on *your* side, she'll saut his purridge Guid an' proper if he entertains the notion Sicc a' pairrin' widna cause a right commotion. Onywey, she'll fyke oot how he feels aboot it And convince the galoot; better dae withoot it! Well, when ah went tae arrange this wee rendezvous Tartuffe's servin' man gie'd me quite a talkin'-to For ettlin' tae disturb Maister ett his Evenin' Prayers. — However, ony meenit noo, he'll be doon the stairs And if you two skedaddle, noo dinnae ask why! Ah'll nab Tartuffe as he goes by.
VALÈRE:	I'll stay right here and grab the devil.
DORINE:	Naw, leave it tae me —
VALÈRE:	I'll be civil!
DORINE:	Civil nothing, you'll lose the heid And that, young lovers, would be a' we need! Get!
MARIANNE:	Valère's right! He'll be diplomatic.
DORINE:	Here he's! Hide! Is this no pathetic?

(SCURRYING ABOUT, DORINE FINALLY GETS VALÈRE INTO ONE CUPBOARD, MARIANNE INTO ANOTHER)

Scene Two

(ENTER TARTUFFE FOLLOWED BY HIS MAN, LAURENT. PERCEIVING AN AUDIENCE IN DORINE HE ACTS UP TO IT.)

TARTUFFE:	Laurent! Awa' an' lock up ma King James Bible. An' bring me linament — Ah'm awfy liable Tae rheumaticks wi' bein' so lang oan the caul' flair, kneelin'. It sterts wi peens an' needles then Ah lose a' feelin' . . . It's gi'ein' me gyp, so git thon embrocation — Och an' pit ma bookmerk in whaur Ah wis readin: *Lamentations!* *"How doth the city sit solitary that was full of people!* *How is she become a widow she that was great among* *the nations and princess among the provinces, how* *is she become a tributary . . . The Lord hath accomplished*

30

TARTUFFE: cont.	*his fury . . . They that were brought up in scarlet shall* *embrace dunghills . . ."*
DORINE:	(ASIDE) "Laurent! Knot ma scourge again, mak' shair it hurt. An' hem an extra awfy jaggy bit on ma hairshirt." Whit a big ham! He must think Ah'm green. (ALOUD) Excuse me!
TARTUFFE:	(ASIDE) Well, yon's a sich fur richt sair een! (ALOUD) Ach, *chist* a minute there, Ah'll thank yi Afore ye speak tae me tae tak' this hanky In the name o' a' that's holy and religious —
DORINE:	Whit fur?
TARTUFFE:	To cover up yir . . . yir . . . whidjies. It's evil sichts lik' yon, I'm sure it is. That swall men's thochts wi' impurities.
DORINE:	You must be awfy fashed wi' flesh tae fire Yir appetites sae quick wi' Base Desire. As fur masel', Ah'm no that easy steered. If you were barescud-nakit, aye and geared Up guid and proaper, staunin' hoat for houghmagandie I could lukk and lukk ett you, and no get randy.
TARTUFFE:	You should wash oot that mooth wi soap! Ah'm going. you'll repent, I hope.
DORINE:	No, *Ah'm* away, but first of all: My mistress asked me to ask you could she pay a call? — With all respect, sir, its a maitter of some delicacy . . . Would you kindly grant her an audience just now, in privacy . . .
TARTUFFE:	Oh but maist certainly!
DORINE:	(ASIDE) As nice as pie! Ah think Ah was right the furst time, aye . . .
TARTUFFE:	Will she be long?
DORINE:	Doon these stairs will come, wha else, Elmire. I'll lea' yiz by yir ain twa sel's.

(EXIT DORINE PANTOMIMING AS MUCH AS POSSIBLE RE THE
TRUTH OF THE RUMOURS TO THE ENTERING ELMIRE, THEN
TRYING TO DISGUISE IT AS AN ITCH AS TARTUFFE CATCHES
HER AT IT. SHE SCURRIES OFF.)

31

Scene Three

TARTUFFE: May merciful heaven grant to thee and thine
Health, wealth and grace baith temporal and divine.
I, God's humblest servant ask, and ask in all sincerity,
May He crown you all your days wi' bountiful prosperity.

ELMIRE: I'm much obliged, you're far too kind, now please
Let's sit down and be a wee bit more at ease . . .

TARTUFFE: Ah trust you are nae longer . . indisposed?

ELMIRE: I'm fine. It was jist a wee virus, I suppose.

TARTUFFE: God's guid indeed, that he should grant
Tae me, a miserable sinner a' Ah want —
For ma every desire in prayer and supplication
Was for your Guild Health and Total Restoration.

ELMIRE: Thank you, but such concern's, I'm sure, excessive —

TARTUFFE: Noo that's impossible, in earnestness Ah've
Begged the Lord tae spare your health and tak' ma ain.

ELMIRE: I'm sure such useless sacrifice were no one's gain —
— I'm very grateful, though, to you . . .

TARTUFFE: Sich loving-kindness is only what you're due.

ELMIRE: There's a certain wee something — Can I bend your ear?
It's . . . fortunate we're so private and secluded here . . .

TARTUFFE: Alane wi' you at last — I'm quite delightit.
And very gled oor pleasure's mutual and requitit!
Ah've often intercedit wi' the Lord fur sich a circumstance
But heaven, till noo, 's denied tae me the chance.

ELMIRE: — Speaking as (to all intents and purposes) Marianne's
mother . . .
Mr. Tartuffe, can we be . . . open and unbuttoned with each
other?

TARTUFFE: My dearest wish, Mistress, is to lay bare
My hert and soul — incidentally, I swear
What you micht, erronously, have thocht was me criticizin'
The company you keep — actually this lies in
A zeal for *you*, in case you're misinterpreted.
Were they to cry you "scarlet wummin" I'd see red!
In fact I'd —

ELMIRE: It's easy to tell fair
From false, and know who's for your welfare —

(HE PRESSES THE ENDS OF HER FINGERS)

TARTUFFE: Right you are, pre-*zactly*, and needless to say —

ELMIRE: Ooyah, you're nipping!

TARTUFFE: I got carried away!
Ah'd dee raither than hurt you, Ah care faur
Too much to ever —

(HIS HAND HAS DROPPED TO HER KNEE)

ELMIRE: What's your hand down there for?

TARTUFFE: An *awfy* bonny frock, it mak's you every inch a lady
Ah wiz fair . . . ta'en up wi' seein' whit it's made y!
Ah canny tell felt fae velveteen you see!

(ELMIRE REMOVES HAND DEFTLY)

ELMIRE: The *dress* is velvet, the only thing that's felt's ma knee.

(MOLIÈRE'S DIRECTION: SHE PUSHES BACK HER CHAIR AND
TARTUFFE DRAWS HIS NEARER)

TARTUFFE: (GAWPING DOWN ELMIRE'S CLEAVAGE & FINGERING THE LACE
AT THE NECKLINE)
Goodness gracious, when you lukk intae it
The lacey-work they're daein nooadays is awfy intricate!
I can't imagine onythin' pit together better.

ELMIRE: Right enough, but about this Other Metter . . .
They say my husband's going to break his word and you
And my stepdaughter are to marry . . . Is this true?

(IN UNISON, BEHIND THEM, FIXED ON ELMIRE AND TARTUFFE,
VALÈRE SLOWLY STICKS HIS HEAD OUT AND MARIANNE,
LISTENING)

TARTUFFE: Wee skliff o' a lassie — och he did mention
The ghost o' the idea, but Ah've nae intention —
Confidentially, elsewhere than in a mairriage wi' a wean
Lies the Blissful Ecstacy I hope I micht attain.

ELMIRE: That's because your minds on Higher Things, you're not
As Other Men —

TARTUFFE: — Ma hert's no made of stone ye ken —

ELMIRE: — And your longings are so spiritual and high you
Know that nothing in this world can satisfy you.

33

TARTUFFE: On the contrary, the quest for godliness
             Shouldnae mak' us love the world the less.
             It's His Creation cherms oor senses, which is only right
             Because God made the world for oor delight.
             The pleasure o' the sicht, say, o' some wummin who is
                                                    Really Nice
             Is the nearest glimpse us pair, vile men get o' paradise.
             So, perfect creature, when you ken you are adored
             Ken tae that in adorin' you I praise the Lord.
             Aye, ma hert's transported, I am dazzled by your beauty!
             Noo, at furst Ah hud tae ask masel, as wis ma duty,
             Wis ah quite, quite shair this wee saicret tenderness
             Wisnae mibbe yin o' Auld Nick's ploys, to land me in a mess?
             Aye, Ah wiz feart you bein' sae . . . Nice Tae Lukk Ett
             Wiz as a mote in ma e'e and Ah'd better pluck it
             Oot, in case it staun atween me an' Salvation
             As ony kinna stumblin' block. — Better, faur better than
                                                    Damnation
             Wad be Ah'd flee fae you, ma yin Temptation.
             Ah took it tae the Lord. He didny will sic deprivation.
             He kennt Ah'd wrastled an' Ah'd wrastled wi ma passion,
             Hoo Ah'd been up a' nicht on ma knees, fair lashin'
             Masel' wi guilt, an' a' fur whit?
             It could be reconcilt wi' discretion, Ah could gie wey tae it!
             Ah ken, Ah ken, Ah've goat an awfy nerve —
             Backward at comin' furrit as Ah am, Ah dinnae deserve
             Ye'd show a hert o' flesh and bluid to me.
             — Except you are kind . . . and God's aye guid to me . . .
             Madam, Ah'm in your hauns, I'm tormentit!
             Mak' me blissfu', peacefu' an' contentit!
             Ah offer you this beatin' hert, so please yirsel'
             Mak' me the happiest man on earth or dash ma hopes to Hell.

ELMIRE: You are most . . . gall*ant*, but this declaration
             Causes me great surprise, if not consternation —
             You should have been a mite more guarded, sir, and thought
             About the implications of such a plot.
             You! Piety is your middle name!

TARTUFFE: Oh aye, Ah'm mibbe holy, but Ah'm human a' the same.
             It's you! Yir . . . celestial cherms are sae owerwhelmin'ly
                                                    tremendous
             The hert kens nae reason, an' surrenders.
             Noo, if such language micht sound strange Ah'll
             Be the first tae admit it: Ah'm nae angel,
             An' afore ye blame me, ye micht just as well
             Blame yir ain enticin' weys, ya lovely Jezebel,

34

TARTUFFE:
cont.

Yir comehither lukks, yir kennin' glances an' yir smiles.
Och, normally Ah'm proof against sicc female wiles.
F'r instance tak' the likes o' yir stepdaughter!

(HE SHAKES HIS HEAD AND MARIANNE PEEKS OUT MAD,
LISTENING)

Ah could pass lang 'oors alane wi her an' nae thought a
Ever even thinkin' o' her as a wummin!
Pair Wee Marianne! Nothin' worth bummin'
Aboot in the looks depertment as faur as Ah cin see!
An' yit she fairly loves hersel', it's "Lukk ett me,
Ah'm jist gorgeous, Ah'm Ah no' the Bees' Knees?"
Fact is, some men urrny hard tae please.
Ony wee straight-up-and-doon skelf in a skirt's
Enough fur them — if she giggles an' flirts
An' wiggles an' flatters an' bats her een
An' greases up her lips wi' vaseline.
Skinnymalinky so-ca'd flappers canny haud a caunle
Tae a real wummin lik' you, yir too hoat tae haunle
— Ma angel, ma ice-maiden, ma fountain o' virtue!
Tak' peety on me an' ye cin bet yir shirt you
An' yir precious reputation will be safe wi' me.
A' they mashers an' gigolos, yi cin guarrantee
They'll boast an' brag aboot yi, they'll kiss an' tell
Wi' who, an' hoo minny times, an' hoo well!
Here's ma warnin' — an' it canny be too strongly worded —
What they kid-oan they worship, they mak' sordid.
But People Like Us, we're mair discreet
We're gey carefu' to guerd oor sweet
Ladies sweet nothin's, an' their sweet sumthin's tae —
— Well, oor *Ain* Good Names are, needless to say,
Things we must, at a' cost, tak' guid care y!
So, kiss me in confidence, dinny be wary!
An' Ah promise tae you, a' ma life lang, ma dear,
Love withoot Scandal, Joy without Fear.

ELMIRE:

I hear what you're saying, but if I took the notion
To acquaint my husband with your . . . declared devotion
Wouldn't he feel betrayed by the man who so rewards him
For all the generous friendship he's shown towards him?

TARTUFFE:

Naw, naw, ye're faur too nice, you winnae!
Ah ken you ken yirsel' the flesh is weak, noo dinnae —!
Funn yirsel' a mirror, lukk lang an' deep in
An' mind that a man is jist a man — unless he's blin'.

ELMIRE:

Others might look at this differently . . .
But, on reflection, mibbe I'll go gently —
Not clype to my husband, let's say Ah'll

35

ELMIRE: Keep mum about your proposition and betrayal
cont. If — and only if — you do all you can
To hasten the wedding of Valère and Marianne
And openly denounce the power which would entrust
You with what belongs to someone else. It's unjust!
And . . .

Scene Five

(MARIANNE BEHIND THEM IS SHAKING HER CROSSED FINGERS
AND SIGNALLING DELIGHT AT ELMIRE'S WILES AS VALÈRE THE
FOOLHARDY MORAL ARBITER LEAPS OUT SHE DUCKS
CRINGING BACK OUT OF SIGHT)

VALÈRE: I think it's time we spilt the beans!
I'm stuck here listening all the time this scene's
Unfolding and at first I can't believe my ears!
And then the penny drops. It clicks. Now here's
Our opportunity! Tartuffe's comeuppance!
He gave us it on a plate, I don't give tuppence
— Now he's blotted his copybook on every page —
For his chances of avoiding Orgon's rage.

ELMIRE: No Valère. It is enough he mends his ways so
He deserves forgiveness by doing my say-so,
Remember? Propositions! A woman of the world'll just
ignore them
And keep from her husband what'll only bore him.

(MARIANNE JUMPS OUT OF HIDING PLACE AND RUNS TO
VALÈRE'S SIDE, HAVING JACKED UP HER LOYALTY)

MARIANNE: Valère's right!

ELMIRE: (ASIDE) Oh no!

VALÈRE: I'm sure you have your reasons
But now he's shown his colours, well the season's
Ripe for showing him his sun is set. It
Is all up, the party's over, sonny, don't forget it!
The cat's out of the bag, the truth's out of the closet
We'll open Orgon's eyes, Bob's your uncle, easy does it!
Don't beg or plead, Tartuffe, there is no use,
You've burnt your boats and cooked your goose.
Fate's dealt me a trump card. Oh ya beauty!
And I'll damn well play it. It is my duty.

ELMIRE: Valère . . .

MARIANNE: Valère's right!

ELMIRE: Marianne . . .

VALÈRE: I must
Inform Orgon Tartuffe's betrayed his trust.

Scene Six

(ENTER ORGON)

MARIANNE: Here's daddy now!

VALÈRE: C'mere, sir, till we tell you
Something very rich! You should know how well you
Are paid back for your generosity.
Your kindness to certain strangers has earned a fine
reciprocity!

He reveals a zeal that's real, Tartuffe!
He wanted to betray you and I've got proof.
The worst bad black villain ever born's Tartuffe.
He would have had you wearing horns, Tartuffe
Would! I sat in that cupboard and I overheard
Him declare a filthy guilty passion to Elmire, every word!
Your easy-going wife would keep it secret; she doesn't want
To upset *you,* and she's so . . . tolerant.
But — the cheek of him! — I can't go along
With just-ignore-it! To shut up'd be wrong.

MARIANNE: Valère's right!

ELMIRE: The way I see it, the big mistake's
To worry one's old man with every passing pass that someone
makes.

I know I'm faithful, so why go in for sessions
Of No Kiss, But Still Tell All True Confessions?

(TURNING TO MARIANNE ALTHOUGH ONCE AGAIN IT'S VALÈRE
WHO GOES TO PROTEST OUT LOUD)

You and your big mouth, miss, we'd have avoided this to-do
If I had more influence over you!

(ITCHING TO SLAP HER)

ORGON: Whit? In the name o' God can this be possible?

37

TARTUFFE: Yes, brither, it is — is this no terrible?
Of a' sinners Ah am maist mizzrable.
Ah cairry a ton weight o' stinkin' guilt that's truly horrible.
Ah'm wicked, proud and fu' o' iniquitousness.
Ah'm corrupted, Ah'm polluted, ma hale life is a mess.
Thank you heaven! Ah see ye mean tae mortify me
An' fur ma ain guid show me whit's fur me'll no go by me.
Ah tell you, whether crime or error or jist faux-pas
Ah'm guilty. Mea absolutely culpa.
So tak' up erms, Orgon, an drive me fae yir door as
Despised as rejectit as Nebbuchadnezzar on a' fours.
Ah'm totally ashamed. Eftir a' you did for me
Nae punishment's enough, hanging's too guid for me.

ORGON: (TO VALÈRE)
See! Ya snake-in-the gerss ye! Ye dampt *disease!*
Hoo daur ye try an' blacken Him wi' yir damnable lees?

TARTUFFE: Orgon, Orgon, ye should listen to the boay!
No' a bit o' malice in him, Ah'm shair he'd no enjoy
Pittin' ye right aboot ma wrang-daein'.
Dinny believe in me, d'ye ken whit yir sayin'?
Don't jist trust ma fine exterior, Ah'd be a hypocrite
If Ah kidded-oan ah wis perfect an' didny admit
Ah'm capable o' vile treachery — which, God willin',
Ah'll no' get away wi'. Unmask me as a villain.
Fur Ah'm nothin' mair nor less, whitever folk think.
The truth o' the maitter is : Ah stink.

(TARTUFFE SINKS TO HIS KNEES)

ORGON: That's too much brither! (TO VALÈRE) Ya . . Ya . . take back
thae lies!

VALÈRE: It's that easy to pull the wool down over your eyes?

ORGON: Shut it ya — Och, brither, up ye get!
Ya — och, see you, ya —

VALÈRE: It's absurd! I've got proof, don't
forget.

ORGON: Wan mair word fae you an' Ah'll brekk yir boady!

TARTUFFE: Dinnae, brither, dinnae, ah'll tak' the hale load y
Righteous anger on ma wicked shooders, d'ye no' see
Ah couldny staun tae see him suffer ower me?

ORGON: Oh! ya —

TARTUFFE: Forgi'e him, forgi'e him! If Ah've tae grovel
in a midden
And beg on ma hauns and knees till —

ORGON: Are you kiddin'?
          Ya tyke, ye! See hoo guid he is!

VALÈRE: Then you —

ORGON: Don't dare
                                                abuse him!
          Easy seein' yir motives, Ah ken how ye accuse him!
          Yiz hate him! Ye dae, the hale dampt loat —
          Wife, dochter, servants in wan big ploat
          Tae discredit this . . . Saint here an' drive him away.
          Ah'll keep him at my richt haun whitever yiz say.
          Ah'll pit furrit the date, gi'e him ma dochter's haun'
          Ah'm all for Tartuffe, an' Ah'll mak' yiz unnerstaun —

VALÈRE: You'd force him on her, you're that twisted and bitter?

ORGON: Aye, ya bliddy rascal, afore she kens whit's hit her
          She'll be Mrs Tartuffe. This vera nicht.
          That'll soart the loat o' yiz oot, a' richt!
          Ah'll show yiz all Ah'm still the boss.
          Doon oan yir knees you — Ah'll no argue the toss —
          Dae it! Tak' it a' back, on yir bended knees,
          And beg him to forgive you please.

VALÈRE: Him? Who except for swindling's never done a thing for you —

ORGON: A stick! Gie's a stick, by God Ah'll swing for you!
          Get oot o' here, an' never have the neck tae show yir face.

VALÈRE: Awright, Ah'll go, but listen —

ORGON: Get oot o' ma place!
          Get oot all o' yiz, the quicker Ah see the back o' yiz
          The better! Ah'll be revenged on the pack o' yiz!

          (ORGON BEGINS TO SWIPE & SWAT EVERYONE AWAY EXCEPT
          TARTUFFE, WHO WITH ONE EYE ON THIS & A TRIUMPHANT
          SMIRK HE CAN'T TOTALLY SUPPRESS SINKS TO HIS KNEES AND
          BEGINS BABBLING MORE *LAMENTATIONS*)

TARTUFFE: *"They ravished the women in Zion and the maids in the cities
          of Judah! The elders have ceased from the gate the young men
          from their music. The joy of our heart is ceased, our dance is
          turned into mourning. Servants have ruled over us and we
          have none that deliver us out of their hand."*

Scene Seven

(THEY ARE ALONE IN QUIET AT LAST)

ORGON: Tae insult yir Holy Name, ah'm black affronted!

TARTUFFE: Heaven forgive them, the last thing Ah've wanted
Is tae be the inadvertant cause o' a' this fuss.
They wey they try an' blacken me, an' come atween us . . .

ORGON: Dinnae!

TARTUFFE: The vera thocht o' sicc ungratefu'ness!
. . . Tae come face to face lik' that wi' Man's Vile Black
            hatefu'ness . . .
The horror! It's sic torture tae me . . .
Ma hert's ower fu' tae talk, Ah'll dee!

(ORGON RUNS TO THE DOOR AND SHOUTS AFTER HIS FUTURE
SON-IN-LAW (REJECTED))

ORGON: Ya villain! (Tae think Ah let him go as well!)
Come back here till ah send ye tae hell!
Pey nae attention tae him, brither, dinnae fash yirsel —

TARTUFFE: Naw, Ah've ootsteyed ma welcome, Ah cin tell.
Ah've caused a lot o' bother, and sich rows —
By faur the best thing fur it is Ah leave this house.

ORGON: Whit? you're kiddin on —

TARTUFFE: They hate me!
They try 'n' arouse yir suspicions jist to bait me.

ORGON: Them an' their rubbish, Ah cin dae withoot it!

TARTUFFE: They'll persist wi' it, but, nae doot aboot it.
An' eftir the umpteenth time they've said it
Ah think ye'll begin tae gie their slanders credit.

ORGON: Naw, brither, naw.

TARTUFFE: Aye brither, aye
It's the wife that weers the breeks in here, that's why.

ORGON: Nut at a'!

TARTUFFE: Let me leave here on the double,
Sharpish — afore they cause me further trouble . . .

ORGON: By God ye'll stey, Ah couldny live wi' sic a loss —

TARTUFFE: Och well ah suppose Ah'll huv tae bear ma cross . . .
Hooever . . .

40

ORGON: Eh?

TARTUFFE: A'richt, so be it!
But we'll huv tae soart things oot . . . The wey Ah see it . . .
Ah'll stey but Ah cin only stey oan wan condition.
We've tae no jist *be* but be-seen-to-be above suspicion.
So, tae stap the waggin' tongues, upon ma life,
There's some'dy Ah'll shun lik' the plague — your wife.

ORGON: Naw ye willny, jist t'annoy them, jist fur spite
Ye'll see her morning noon an' night.
But that's no a'. Ah'll chinge ma will —
Soart ma cheeky bitch o' a daughter, if she's still
Under the illusion that she cin defy me,
Well, Ah've the whip haun', she'll be taught a lesson by me.
Ah'll mak' you ma yin an' only heir
So she'll mairry you or starve. An' furthermair
Why wait till Ah'm deid? Whit mair dae Ah want
Ah'll make everythin' ower tae you the now, by deed o'
                                         covenant!
Whit di' you think o' that, eh, then?

TARTUFFE: Even so, Lord, Thy will be done, then . . . Amen.

ORGON: Pair sowell! Well, let's pit oor signatures on the page . . .
They'll be seeck! They'll be green! They'll burst wi' rage!

(MUSIC OF A FANFARE NATURE AND JUBILANT ORGON INSISTS
ON TARTUFFE SIGNING, THEM EXCHANGING PAPERS &
SHAKING HANDS. OF COURSE ORGON LOSES HIS FOUNTAIN PEN
TO THE VILLAIN AS WELL, AS OFF GOES THE POOR DUPE
LOOKING QUITE DELIGHTED WITH HIMSELF. TARTUFFE IS
TOO, NOW WE HAVE HIM ALONE AND HE CAN INDULGE IT. HE
LOOKS ROUND, MONARCH OF ALL HE SURVEYS, SLIDES HIS
HANDS OVER VELVET UPHOLSTERY, GLOATING, AND SITS
DOWN DRUMMING HIS HEELS IN DELIGHT AND LAUGHING
LIKE A MANIAC AS THE CURTAIN FALLS.)

END OF MOLIÈRE'S ACT THREE

END OF *OUR* FIRST ACT. INTERVAL.

Act Four: Scene One

(ENTER CLÉANTE TO FIND TARTUFFE QUIET, WHERE WE LEFT HIM.)

CLÉANTE: Ah, very timely! Mr Tartuffe, upon my life
Everybody's talking — the world and his wife
Is quite scandalised by this — I hope it's untrue? —
Otherwise it reflects most unfavourably on you.
Maybe Valère's a hothead — perhaps mistaken, granted!
— Certainly he was overquick accusing you in a way that no
                                                    one wanted —
But surely to goodness the Christian thing
Is to pardon what seems beyond pardonning?
Because of a wee falling-out he's banished, is it fair?
The boy who was the future-son-in-law, the heir —
— Until Orgon capriciously went back on his word.
People are, I repeat, outraged by it — it'd be absurd
If it weren't so patently and painfully unjust.
Here's my advice, sir, and you'll take it I trust?
You're in a position to pour oil on troubled water . . .
Make it all hunky-dory again between father and daughter.
À propos Valère . . . ask God to cleanse you of your —
                                    understandable resentment
And let the young ones get on with it in peace and contentment.

TARTUFFE: Now it's ower and done wi' as faur as Ah'm concerned.
I bear him nae grudge, Ah'm shair he's learned
Repentance, is sorry, could bite his tongue et cetera.
I forgive him, no bother — but Heaven kens it's better Ah
Dinnae be seen tae have ony truck
Wi' the young filla — you're richt — there's muck
In a' their minds an' rumours on their lips
An' their beady een are peeled for ither folk's slips
Or stumbles, backsliding's aff the straight and narra.
Turn the ither cheek? Ah'd be gled tae, but as far a
-S the warld's concerned it'd be as guid as pleading guilty.
                                                    How?
They'd reason it lik' this: Ah wis only actin' pally now
Because Ah wis feart o' ma Just Accuser — that's how they'd
                                                describe him —
An' Ah wis only sufferin' him tae silence and bribe him.

CLÉANTE: Mr. Tartuffe, that's a very colourful excuse.
A mite far-fetched this sophistry, now what's the use
Of taking on your feeble shoulders Heaven's interests

CLÉANTE: Let Heaven punish who It likes, doesn't Heaven know best?
cont. Vengeance is Mine Said the Lord — so let's leave him to it.
Remember, should He choose to forgive, then it's the right
thing to do it.
What should we care for the opinion of some mythical
"them"?
If "they"'re so petty-minded as condemn
A good deed, so twisted as misconstrue our motives
Then let "us" obey Heaven, and if Heaven forgives —

TARTUFFE: Ah tellt you I forgave him and I — don't you understand? —
meant
Jist that. As is the Good Lord's Commandment,
Though Valère reviled and slandered me I forgive the blether.
But heaven kens it isny written we should live the-gether!

CLÉANTE: And is it written sir, that on Orgon's whim
Valère be dispossessed and you should usurp him?
Taking his bride, her inheritance and his good name?
Accepting property to which you have no just claim?

TARTUFFE: Ah jist maun trust that those who ken me best
Ken better than Ah'd act oot o' self interest.
A' the glisterin' riches in the warld mean nut a thing tae me.
Ah'm the last wan tae get dazzled by their glamourie
An' if, against ma inclinations, ah force masel
Tae tak this faither's insistit-oan gifts it's jist as well
Seein' as, otherwise, Ah'm very much feart it's bound to fa'
Inty wicked hauns that willny yase it well at a'!
But I, lik' the guid and faithfu' servant wi his talent, I will
yase it, if Ah can,
For the Glory o' God, the well-bein' o' ma fellow man.

CLÉANTE: Better he misuse it and be answerable to God
Than you be —in error — suspected of fraud,
Sir!

TARTUFFE: Would you look at the time, it's half past three!
A certain religious duty up the stairs, you'll have to be
excusing me —

(EXITS QUICKLY)

CLÉANTE:. Em . . .!

Scene Two

(ENTER ELMIRE AND DORINE WITH WEEPING MARIANNE)

DORINE: Help us sir, for pity's sake!

DORINE:
cont.

Lukk at the state she's in, we huv tae make —
Either by trickin' him or teachin' him sense —
Her faither gie this up! Jine us in defence
O' fair play an' true love against this mess
O' maister's. Sich unhappiness.

Scene Three

(ENTER ORGON)

ORGON:

Och! A' here thegither? That's sweet.
(TO MARIANNE)
Somethin' in these papers, hen, that's right up your street.

MARIANNE:

Father, in the name of anythin' that's sacred to your heart,
or moves you,
For the sake of Heaven, and your own daughter who loves
you,
I beg you, daddy, please, please, you gave me life.
Don't render it a misery to me by making me the wife
Of a man who to even think-of makes my flesh to crawl.
Must I give up my last sweet hope for once and all?

(ORGON IS MOVED. ASIDE, TO HIMSELF)

ORGON:

Be firm! Ever since she wis a toddler she could wrap ye
roon her pinkie!

MARIANNE:

I'm not put-out *you* love him, I think he
Must deserve it, if you think so, fine.
Give him all your money and add what's mine,
It doesn't matter to me, I present
My last trinket, take it, give it with my consent
From the bottom of my heart. And God he
Knows that all I ask's you don't give away my body.
And if I can't marry that one person I love so much
Then let me die a maiden, untouched . . . .

(SHE HAS BOWED HER HEAD DURING LAST SO SHE DOESN'T SEE
THAT ORGON IS REACHING OUT ABOUT TO GIVE WAY TO HER,
SOFTENED UTTERLY)

MARIANNE:

Let me turn Catholic! In God's honour, He
Bids me live my days out in a nunnery.

44

ORGON: Turn whit! Ah think you must be makin' fun o' me!
Ya *get* ye! Ye'll get ye to no nunnery!
Did yir Daddy hear ye say a Catholic Convent? Hih?
                                                    Nae wunner he
Is *forced* tae huv tae run yir life fur ye.
Get oan yir feet! Ah don't know whit tae say!
Maks "yir flesh creep" diz he? Oh aye!
There's ower much concentration on "the flesh" that's why.
That's an end tae it! Forget the flesh's vile gratification,
Mortify yirsel, mairry him an' avoid damnation.

DORINE: But whit —

ORGON: You haid yir tongue! God's truth!
Ah'll . . . Ah'll . . . Jist shut yir mooth.

CLÉANTE: For what it's worth, can I just put in a word —

ORGON: Ha-ha! Your advice, brither, is the best Ah've heard
Ah mean it! Honestly Ah'm grateful for it —
Forgive me though if this once Ah ignore it!

ELMIRE: Enough! I just don't know what to say
Except your wilful blindness takes my breath away.
You must be literally bewitched, quite honestly,
To deny the truth of what occurred today.

ORGON: Ah! Well, Ah'm faur fae blin', unfortunately fur you!
Valère's a nice lukkin' young fella, eh? — sich as you're
                                                    partial to?
Favouratism mak's ye that bit lenient, ye didny want tae
                                                    contradict him
When he tried to play his durty trick wi' Tartuffe for a
                                                    victim.
— But of coorse ma lovely wife would have been *faur* mair
                                                    upset
If a man had *really* made advances tae ma innocent wee pet.

ELMIRE: You wanted me to prudishly pretend to be offended!
I simply laughed it off. My honour's easily defended
Because I'm quite secure in it, my dear.
Some of these spitfires and hysterics doth protest too much,
                                                    I fear.
I find a civilised and cool-but-firm rebuff
Deters unwanted attentions effectively enough.

ORGON: Nevertheless there's naebody gonny tak' a len o' me!

ELMIRE: Hell's teeth! Alright, we'll make you see.

ORGON: See?

45

ELMIRE: Uh-huh, see.

ORGON: Well, Ah'd be seein' things.

ELMIRE: Righto!
Suppose I said I'd prove that it was so?

ORGON: Ah'd say that was a loady —

ELMIRE: What a man! Enough!
Before your very eyes I'll make him do his stuff.
Get him to come here!

DORINE: He isny daft, he
Likely willny let you catch him, he's too crafty —

ELMIRE: Hurt someone where he loves, that's how to really cause
                                              confusion!
Self-love leads easily to self delusion.
So send him down and leave us for a bit —

(SHOOS OUT CLÉANTE, MARIANNE AND DORINE)

Scene Four

ELMIRE: Quick! Pull over that table and get under it.

ORGON: How?

ELMIRE: God help me, so that you can hide.

ORGON: Why in below here?

ELMIRE: . . . If ever a woman had her patience
                                              solely tried . . .
Never mind! A foolproof scheme and you shall be its judge.
Under this table. Keep quiet. Don't budge.

ORGON: Ah look as if Ah'm that daft! O.K. . . Under there . . .

(HE GOES)

ELMIRE: Sweetheart, you'll see me acting sort of strangely I declare
I'm going to do a thing I've never done before in all my life!
Now don't let it shock you, dear, to see a new side of your
                                              wife.
Remember "ends and means" . . . and so on . . . and since you
Refuse to take me at my word I must convince you —
So don't cast it up after! You mustn't disparage

46

ELMIRE: My motives, dearest, if I sort of encourage —
cont.   By buttering him up — you'll see me flirt somewhat and
                                                        flatter . . .
          Oh a dirty trick perhaps, but, no matter
          It was *he* proposed outrageous things to *me!*
          So I'll encourage full expression of his lust and vanity.
          Now it's up to you to call a halt — you'd be more than an
                                                        accessory
          If you let this odious charade last one minute longer than is
                                                        necessary —
          Husht!

Scene Five

(ENTER TARTUFFE)

TARTUFFE: They tell me that you wish to speak with me?

ELMIRE: I do, I do indeed, in secrecy . . .
          Shut the door. That cupboard! We don't want noseyparkers
                                                        check!
          No repetitions of that last fiasco, we got a right rid neck!
          Valère and Marianne landed us right in it, I was worried
                                                        for you!
          I tried to shut him up, I didn't know *what* to do . . .
          I was that vexed at them . . . *confused,* that was why it
          Never even occurred to me to deny it!
          But all's well that ends well, better by far
          My husband himself dismissed it and . . . here we are!
          Alone. With his blessing. Trusted. I'm hoping
          (I blush) we can hide our love affair out in the open?

TARTUFFE: Our love a — whit? Madam, this efternoon
          Ye hud me dancin' tae a different tune.

ELMIRE: Dear Tartuffe, you don't know women, you're so innocent!
          A refusal like that! You surely never thought I meant
          It? We women struggle so with modesty when we transgress
          But you know that we say 'no' when we mean 'yes'!
          (AS HE'S UNCONVINCED SHE'S FORCED TO ELABORATE)
          I spoke a dutiful refusal, as I *know* you realise,
          With a butter-wouldn't-melt mouth, but come-to-bed eyes.
          — I ask you: would I have tried to shush Valère?

47

ELMIRE: cont.	Would I have listened to you so long? And what do you infer From the fact I tried to force you to renounce the marriage But that I basically wanted to encourage You to keep your love intact, and all-for-me, Because I was literally green with jealously?
TARTUFFE:	It's the sweetest thing on earth — thanks be tae heaven above — Tae hear honey love-words fae someb'dy that ye love. Ah never tasted sicc a precious thing afore — Ma yin thocht is tae mak' happy the wummin Ah adore. But — haud oan ma foolish hert! — I hae a lingerin' suspicion — Noo I micht be wrang, but pit yersel in ma position — Whit if Ah break aff the weddin' because Ah believe That you want ma love, then yi laugh up yir sleeve An' it turns oot it wiz jist a ploy? Ah can't 'just trust' in tender words till Ah enjoy Warm livin' breathin' tenderness atween us baith. Kiss me! Quickly! In token of good faith.

(ELMIRE COUGHS A WARNING AT HIDDEN ORGON)

ELMIRE:	Whit! I emm don't think we need move so fast — Too soon spent kisses never last! I promise all the happiness of which you dream's Around the corner, if you don't push it to extremes . . .
TARTUFFE:	It's kennin' ma ain worthlessness mak's me doot That you could ever love me, so withoot You prove yir love in no uncertain fashion Ah canny go a' the wey wi yir words o' passion.
ELMIRE:	Goodness! I love you so it gives me palpitations. My heart is pounding with agitation Of seeing that my churning feelings don't burst their dam! You mustn't take advantage, see how weak I am . . . A mere woman led astray by the man on whom she depended! It'd be quite wrong, heaven would be offended.
TARTUFFE:	Leave it tae me tae square it wi Heaven.
ELMIRE:	It'd be a mortal sin, we'd never be forgiven —
TARTUFFE:	Heaven forbids certain things, oh aye, bit we'd better Mind we're enjoined tae follow the spirit o' the law and no the letter Under certain circumstances these . . . gratifications that I mention Micht be richt — accordin' tae Purity o' Intention.

TARTUFFE:	(ASIDE)
cont.	

And by God Ah'm gonny pure — !! . . . Ma *intentions* are pure
So on ma heid be it, ye cin rest secure —
My that's an awfy cough!

ELMIRE: Yes! It's ticklish!

TARTUFFE: You want a wee boiling tae sook, or a bit o' lickerish?

ELMIRE: It's tiresome right enough, Ah canny seem to shift it.
            My chest's that congested! Take mair than liquorice to lift it!

(SHE PATS AT HER CLEAVEAGE FOR TARTUFFE'S BENEFIT,
COUGHS FOR HER HUSBAND'S)

TARTUFFE: Quite a chest right enough . . .

ELMIRE: Och! It's got me demented!

TARTUFFE: Oh Ah know whit ye mean. Hmm. Well, Ah hope Ah've
                                                          prevented
            You from being a victim of a silly scruple,
            Let me lead ye, be ma mistress, be ma pupil,
            Let me show ye it's the world and its durty mind
            Disapproves o' love! God isny so unkind!

(ELMIRE HAS A FIT OF COUGHING)

ELMIRE: Well it seems I must give in —
            Lie with you in secrecy, and in sin.
            What my old man doesn't *see* , whether it's wrong or right's
            Certainly not going to cause him any sleepless nights.
            Since certain people don't believe in idle words, Mr Tartuffe
            It seems a bit of action'll show you proof,
            (YELLING)
            Like they say, on your head be it.

(LIES BACK ON THE TABLE)

TARTUFFE: (UNDOING TROUSERS AND ROLLING UP HER SKIRT)
            At last! Noo let's get on wi' it!
            Noo Ah take it on masel, as you'll soon see —

(ELMIRE PUSHES HIM OFF)

ELMIRE: Is ma husband in the passage? Check and see!

TARTUFFE: Is he in the whit? Never heed yir man,
            We'll pull a fast one on him if anybody can!
            An richt afore his nose. Clues! They're just ignored!

He's satisfied our only intercourse is . . . quite above board.

(TARTUFFE BANGS OUT LAST ON THE TABLE)

ELMIRE: Nevertheless I'm just not too sure where he is exactly.
Check it out for me . . and mibbe that'll relax me . . .

(TARTUFFE COMPLIES WITH A ROAR OF FRUSTRATION)

Scene Six

(ORGON COMES OUT FROM UNDER THE BOARD)

ORGON: Ah'm — Ah jist canny — who'd've guessed he'd . . .
Whit an abominable man, Ah'm flabbergasted!

ELMIRE: Out so soon? Get back! To avoid any confusion
We'll go all the way to its logical conclusion.

ORGON: Ah'll see him in Hell! Ma wife! Oh no.

ELMIRE: Now it isn't necessarily so!
Misjudging people can be very nasty
And the last thing you ought to be is overhasty.

Scene Seven

(SHE'S PUSHED ORGON TO THE FLOOR, TARTUFFE DOESN'T SEE
HIM, PUSHES ELMIRE BACK, DROPS HIS TROUSERS, HAND ON
HER BREAST OR SOMETHING GROSS.)

TARTUFFE: Ssh! . . .There's neither hide nor hair . . . On top o' me!

(ORGON LEAPS OUT)

ORGON: My wife! My God! It's daylight robbery . . .
You'd marry ma dochter and . . . and . . .My wife!
Ah've aye had ma suspicions but . . . but never in ma life
Have Ah seen sich . . . sich . . . Oh, Treacherous Stuff,
Sir! You've broke ma hert, Ah've seen enough . . .

ELMIRE: I didn't want to, it was a . . . bit
Below the belt but then you asked for it!

50

TARTUFFE: Whit? D'y' really think . . .

ORGON: Ya bliddy louse!
Nut wan word. Get out ma house.

TARTUFFE: Ye talk as ye were the maister! Get oot o' whit?
Whose hoose? It's *ma* hoose, Ah'll mind ye o' it.
— By Christ ye've gone too far.
Ma 'oor is come. My power. Ma risin' star
Is in the Heavens. Ah'll punish ye!
O they shall eat bitter gall who tried to banish me!

(HE EXITS)

Scene Eight

(ELMIRE MANAGES TO GET OUT A FORCED SNIGGER)

ELMIRE: "They shall eat bitter gall!" The cheek of it!

ORGON: Shut yir stupit face, it's nuthin tae laugh ett!

ELMIRE: Why?

ORGON: I see my fault. I've ruined us all.
The deed of covenant . . . My house shall fall.

ELMIRE: The deed of what?

ORGON: It's done. Consumatum est.
Whit am Ah sayin'? A wolf dressed
Up in sheep's claes. That villain's capers
Were jist tae deliberately dae me oot the Secret Papers!

(EXIT ORGON IN TERRIBLE STATE)

Act Five: Scene One

(ELMIRE STANDS SOBBING, ADJUSTING HER DISARRAYED CLOTHING, RELIVING THE DISGUST OF TARTUFFE'S HANDS ON HER, THE HUMILIATION OF HER SEXUAL DECOY ROLE, PUZZLED AT WHAT THE HELL ORGON'S TALKING ABOUT, GETTING MORE ALARMED AS BITS THAT DON'T SOUND GOOD SINK IN.)

ELMIRE: Dorine! Dorine! Oh why's there never anybody when I want Them? Help me . . . Oh God . . . Cléante!

(CLÉANTE ENTERS LEADING A TOTALLY SHATTERED ORGON. SIGNALS SSH!-AND-DON'T-COME-NEAR-US AS ELMIRE STARTS TOWARDS THEM. HE SHAKES HEAD, SIGNALS SHE KEEP QUIET. SHE DOES.)

CLÉANTE: Now we have to think it out, it seems to me
We better analyse alternatives, look at it logically.
What steps? What losses? What possible gains —

ORGON: Above all it's the case, that briefcase contains
Somethin' that could mean the end.
Argas brought me certain papers. Argas, my friend,
The one who was betrayed. Before he fled
He asked me would Ah guard them or his head
Would roll. He trusted me you understand.

CLÉANTE: Why then did you entrust this to another hand?

ORGON: Ah meant it for the best. It was from a sense
Of mibbe no bein' worthy o' this trust Ah went, in
confidence,
An' tellt the hale tale tae that bliddy rascal.
His argument wiz this: "This task'll
Be much better done gin ye gie the boax to me, Tartuffe.
Then ye cin at yince be shair it's safe ablow yir roof
An' at the same time — should snoopers come — deny
Ye huv it in yir possession, with not wan word o' a lie."

CLÉANTE: It looks like you are in it up to here.
This misplaced trust, this deed of gift are both, I fear,
Things you may live long to regret . . .
Still, he's got you by the short-and-curlies don't forget!
So the worst thing we can do is irritate him —
I wish there was some mollifying subterfuge that might
placate him . . .

ORGON: May God damn an' blast an' pit a pox on pious folk.
Ah loathe an' detest them they gie me the boke.

ORGON: cont.	Ah'll "In-the-name-o'-the-faither-son-an'-Holy-Ghost" them!

Ah'll hunt-them-tae-Hell, Ah'll roast them!

CLÉANTE: Orgon, Orgon, is yon no just like you?
Nae moderation in ye, man, you overdo
It all and lose the rag, you make
Yourself ridiculous! You see your big mistake,
You — and you're not the first one — got took in by a fake.
But all pious people aren't imposters for goodness sake!
Oh the con-man may have a silver tongue, but nevertheless
Our better judgement should be a litmus test for phoniness
And if in doubt we ought to hedge our bets
And steer a somewhat middle-course that lets
Time teach us who we ought to trust.
But still I think we ought to err, if err we must,
As you have erred — by being vulernable and risking
Loving your fellow man in a way that's only Christian.

(NO MOLIÈRE SCENE TWO)

Scene Three

(ENTER PERNELLE, MARIANNE, ELMIRE AND DORINE.)

ORGON: Oh naw! Here's ma mither, oh dear oh dear!

PERNELLE: Whit's the maitter, whit's a' this Ah hear?

ORGON: Fine sichts Ah saw wi ma ain twa een
That proved hoo weel peyed back Ah've been
Fur a' ma guidness. Furst Ah took him in,
Fed him, claithed him — if he'd been ma kin
Ah couldny have done mair fur him.
Ah gied him ma ain dochter sae weel did Ah care fur him.
An' — oh the villainy! — Ah trust him wi' ma life
An' the devil tries tae seduce ma wife.
No content wi' this, he wants ma total ruination.
Each weel-meant hansell, each gift, deed or donation
Ah gied him oot the goodness o' ma hert
He wants tae yase against me tae ootsmert
An' swick me oot ma hale estate — you're
Richt, Ah'm a fule tae masel', it is ma nature —
He'll deprive me o' ma last crust o' breid an' butter
An pit me whaur Ah picked him up, the gutter.

DORINE: The sowell.

53

PERNELLE: This Ah don't believe, Ah'll
Never accept That Man could be sae evil.

ORGON: How?

PERNELLE: Guid Folk are ayeweys envied by the ither
Soart, believe me.

ORGON: How d'ye mean, eh, Mither?

PERNELLE: Awfy strange shenanigans ablow this roof.
Easy seein' that they a' hate Tartuffe.

ORGON: Ah'll 'shenanigans' him! Whit justification cin you offer —

PERNELLE: Pure spite! An' aye the innocent must suffer.
The jealous may perish — lik' Ah says when you were wee —
But The Auld Green Eyed Monster Will Never Ever Dee.

ORGON: Whit huz that tae dae wi' it? Who's jealous?

PERNELLE: The loat o' them. Made the hale thing up. Pure malice.

ORGON: Ah seen it wi' ma ain twa een! God gi'e me strength . . .

PERNELLE: Scandalmongerin' slanderers wid go tae ony length.

ORGON: Huv yi loast yir senses a' thegither?
Ah seen him. Richt afore ma very eyes. D'ye hear me
                                        mither?
Ah saw it all. Whit cin Ah say? Must Ah shout
At the tap o' ma voice afore ye tak' in whit Ah'm talkin'
                                        about?
Ah saw him. Ah saw him — wi' these twin undimmed orbèd
                                        optics
I perceived the visual proof to satisfy a school of sceptics.

PERNELLE: You shouldny judge by appearances you know!
Jist 'cos ye thocht ye saw somethin' disnae prove that it wis so.

ORGON: Gie me strength!

PERNELLE: We're prone to suspicion, son — it's gey
Easy tae tak' somethin' the wrang wey!

ORGON: Coorse, it wis jist his guid deed o' the day, and how,
Tae try 'n seduce Ma Wife —

PERNELLE: Now, now!
Just cause afore ye accuse folk, or it isny fair!
Never open yir mooth in anger until ye urr quite shair.

ORGON: Shair! Should Ah huv jis stood by while he dragged her
Doon tae his vile Level, upped her skirt and — shairly
Ye dinna think Ah'd accuse the man unfairly?

54

PERNELLE:	Ah jist cannot accept he is to blame For whit you say! Pair man, it is a shame —
ORGON:	Enough! If you were not ma mither, Ah'd . . . Ah'd . . . Ah'd Ah-don't-know-whit, you make me that mad!
DORINE:	It's jist your Just Desserts, it shouldny grieve you. You wouldny believe us, so why should she believe you?
CLÉANTE:	We're wasting time on all this piffle! What your forgettin's How daft it is to fight amongst ourselves while danger threatens.
ELMIRE:	Danger! The man's a mere balloon! In short Even he couldn't be that blatant, he'd be laughed out of court!
CLÉANTE:	I don't think we can afford to be confident in our position. If he wants to get legal he's got plenty ammunition. Many's the man with a case less cut-and-dried Has bankrupted another with the law on his side. We should've kept in his good books at all cost and not Pushed him so far — with the cards that *he's* got!
ORGON:	That's true.. Ah ken. But it wisnae a maitter O being in control when Ah seen that traitor —
CLÉANTE:	I know, I know! I wonder is there any use In negotiating, somehow, between you some sort of truce?
ELMIRE:	I'd never have dangled myself like a carrot If I'd known exactly the stick *he* had to wield and how far it All might go, oh —
	(KNOCK KNOCK KNOCK PAUSE KNOCK KNOCK KNOCK)
ORGON:	Whit next? Who the hell can that be? Awa' an tell them yir maister's in nae fit state tae talk tae anyb'dy.

Scene Four

(MR LOYAL FOOT IN THE DOOR AS DORINE OPENS IT)

LOYAL:	Mr Orgon? Live here, diz he? Can I have a word, please —
DORINE:	Maister's busy.
LOYAL:	I'd be the last person to intrude On a man in his ain hame. Yir maister should

LOYAL:	Be quite pleased tae hear whit Ah huv tae say.
cont.	Nothin' he'll feel put-oot aboot, anyway . . .
DORINE:	And yir name, sir?
LOYAL:	On behalf of Mr. Tartuffe, I would
	Like a wee word wi' your good maister, f'r his own good.
DORINE:	He's a man who seems to be wan o' nature's gentlemen
	Here fae Who-D'ye-Cry-Him-Again?
	— On business which he says'll please ye.
CLÉANTE:	Wonder what he wants? Best if he sees you . . .
ORGON:	Mibbe he's here tae redd it up an' sort it . . .
	Hoo cin his favour best be courtit?
CLÉANTE:	Now no resentment, keep your hair on, and in his eyes
	Such moderation might encourage him to compromise.
LOYAL:	Good day to you and yours, maister, your servant I'm sure.
	Herm to those that'd herm ye, and may Heaven secure
	Every blessin' on yir house and name and, don't forget,
	We never died o' winter yet.
ORGON:	This filla couldnae be mair civil in his greetin'!
	Mibbe eftur a' we can hae some kinna hauf wey meetin' . . .
LOYAL:	Ah meet ye at last, sir. There wis naebody Ah'd raither
	Dae business wi than your auld dad. Aye! Ah kennt
	yir faither.
ORGON:	Ah thocht Ah kennt yir face . . . but tae ma shame
	Ah don't think ah cin place yir name . . .?
LOYAL:	My name is Loyal — and don't get huffy sir
	When Ah tell you Ah am, by profession, a Sherriff's Officer
	Who has for forty years held this position, tae ma credit,
	And is here today to serve you wi' a writ.
ORGON:	A whit?
LOYAL:	Noo, noo dinny get excited!
	Dinnae loss the heid! That's no how wrongs git righted.
	This is nothing but a mandate of citation
	Ordering you leave your abode or habitation,
	Aforesaid, without delay, with no right of appeal.
ORGON:	Leave ma hoose? Please God this isny real . . .
LOYAL:	Noo, sir, yir hoose,grounds an'every stick o' furniture
	ablow this roof
	As ye ken very well, belangs, nae question, tae Tartuffe.
	Signed and sealed sir, in this document which Ah canny
	help admirin'

56

LOYAL:
cont.

For its legal phrasin'. It's — in layman's terms —
cast iron.

DORINE:

Pit a man oot his ain hoose? That's great, you're
Obviously Loyal by name, hih, an' Loyal by nature.

LOYAL:

Noo Ah dinny see why he tak's it personal an' lukks a' victim
An' longfaced aboot it! Because Ah'm here tae evict him
In as pleasant a manner as is, under difficult circumstances,
possible.
Ah asked tae deliver this personally, because ah thocht
it'd be terrible
If, no' bein' (as Ah like tae think o' masel') a freen' o'
the fam'ly
The deliverin' officer micht *no'* go softly-softly an'
approach it calmly . . .

ORGON:

There is nae saftenin' o' the cruelest blow.
Tae pit a man oot his ain hame!

LOYAL:

Ah'll gi'e ye time ye know.
Ah'll suspend proceedin's, under ma right o' discretion,
And wait till the morra afore Ah take possession.
Okey-dokey. Oh . . . Ah'll hiv tae come an' spend the night
Wi aboot ten o' ma men, ken . . . but they'll be polite!
Nane o' yir rough-stuff, ye'll no ken they're there.
Coorse, ye'll hae tae haun' ower the keys. Tae me. Bit
Ah'll tak' care
There'll be nut a dicky-bird tae disturb yir last night's rest.
But the morn's mornin'. The flittin'. It'd be for the best
If ye'd a' a wee hand-bag packed wi some personal effects,
Items o' essential clothin', etcetra . . . Ah hope naebody
suspects
Tartuffe o' itemising every last crumb or lentil —
Help yirsel' oot the larder! An' tak the odd geegaw o'
sentimental
Value — jist check it oot wi me furst — we'll no be hard.
Ma men are a' big strong boays, they'll help ye cairry!
Well, a bodyguard-
Joab lik' theirs means big broad shooders come in
convenient . . .
Now, as Ah'm shair ye appreciate, Ah've been very lenient
An' treated you, *Ah* feel, mair than fairly.
So Ah cin expect, in return, a bit o' co-operation, shairly?

ORGON:

Co-operwhit? Ah mibbe dinny hae a bean
Tae cry my ain, but Ah tell you Ah mean
Tae git revenge. Ah'd gie a' ma wealth-that-was
Tae brekk yir jaw and kick yir —

57

CLÉANTE: Wheesht, you'll make things worse —

DORINE: Because
Ah'm a wummin doesny mean ma fingers urny itchin' fur a
                                                     stick,
Or Ah dinny notice hoo yir erse is the right shape fur a kick!

LOYAL: Because yir a wummin disny mean that yir above the law.
Git tae vote, eh? Well, ye git tae go tae jile an a'.

CLÉANTE: Enough of all this! Stop it. Cease . . .
Serve your damned paper sir, and leave us in peace.

LOYAL: Cheerio. For the present. May God give you grace.

(EXIT LOYAL)

ORGON: May he damn you and the man who sent you to this place.

Scene Five

ORGON: Wis Ah right or wis Ah wrang, eh Mither?
This treachery must convince ye o' the ither,
An' shairly even you'll admit at last thit —

PERNELLE: Ah've seen it a'. Ah'm flabbergastit.

DORINE: I'm sure ye shouldny blame him, this is proof
O' hoo benevolent is Mister Tartuffe.
He only means it fur the best!
He kens hoo riches are an awfy fikey test
O' a yince guid man's uncorruptibility,
So he kindly took upon hissel the responsibility! —
He wantit you in the Kingdom o' Heaven, that's why!
An' no wi' yir hump stuck like a camel in a needle's eye.

ORGON: Haud yir tongue! If Ah've tellt yi wance, for pity's sake.

CLÉANTE: Let us decide what course tae take . . .

EILMIRE: As far as I can see the whole thing's preposterous!
Such blatant injustice can be no threat to us!
If he were successful it'd cause a public stink.
Or else the law's a far greater ass, even, than I think.

Scene Six

(ENTER VALÈRE)

VALÈRE: This is very urgent, or, believe me, I'd not disturb you.
I've just heard something which will perturb you
I'm sure, as it did me. A certain friend of mine, in fact
Someone who knows you too, in defiance of the Official
                                              Secrets Act
At great risk to himself, leaked certain information
On the strength of which a permanent vacation
Might seem more than desirable. Don't pack, just go.
Certain charges have been brought, you ought to know,
Against you specifically by that bloody imposition
And imposter who you loved. Murmurs of sedition
Were poured in the ears of certain high heid yins,
Papers produced belonging to a Known State Criminal whose
                                              allegiance
Is *not* to our democratic way of life, to say the least.
Tartuffe maintains you harboured this beast,
Helped him escape, concealed for him a certain object
— Namely that box of documents — as no loyal subject
Of Mr. Prince or our proud nation ever would.
I don't know the ins-and-outs but there's a warrant out, it
                                              could
Be that you're accused of a very serious crime indeed.
And, all the better to arrest you, Tartuffe's going to lead
The arresting officer here to execute his
Warrant and fulfil his duties.

CLÉANTE: He's got all the ammunition he needs. That's how the
                                              impostor
Will strip you of everything and make himself master.

ORGON: I tell you that man is a vile, vile creature . . .

VALÈRE: By God you're right! Tartuffe, I hate your
Stinking guts, let me get one punch, I'll kill you —

MARIANNE: Valère shut up and save my father, will you?

VALÈRE: Yes. Quick. Delay is fatal, it's all arranged,
A car outside with its engine running, I've changed
As much currency as I could possibly muster.
They're hot on our heels but we'll be faster.
There's a time to fight, but now's a time to run.
We'll get you to some safe place-in-the-sun.

VALÈRE: No arguments, father, I'm going too.
cont.   If it's to the ends of the earth, I'll see it through.

ORGON: My boay, should Ah survive a' this Ah owe it
            A' tae you. Ah'm sorry. Ah'm thankfu' — but Ah canny
                                                        show it
            In ony usefu' wey unless Heaven grant
            Me someday the chance to gi'e you a' ye want.
            Tak' guid care noo, all o' yiz —

CLÉANTE: Quick, run
            We'll see to everything that must be done.

Last Scene

TARTUFFE: Tooch-tooch, Ah widnae get a jildy oan . . .
            New ludging's ready for you and you alone . . .
            You're for the jile, by order o' Mr. Prince hissel'.

ORGON: This is the unkindest cut o' all.
            Ya devil, the worst thing I could o' askit
            Fur, this fairly tak's the biscuit.

TARTUFFE: In the name o' Heaven, Ah jist let this vile attack
            'N abuse roll aff, watter aff a duck's back.

CLÉANTE: How moderate! I do admire such restraint.

VALÈRE: He bandies Heaven's name aboot, but holy he aint!

TARTUFFE: Neither Heaven nor me's bothered by yir dog's abuse.
            Ah'm only keen tae serve my country and be o' use.

MARIANNE: "Serve your country." Tall order, but then
            Aren't you the best and noblest citizen!

TARTUFFE: Tall order nut-at-all! An honour, a glory, tae obey
            The authority an' power that sends me here the day.

ORGON: Ungratefu' tyke-ye, tae bite the haun that fed ye.
            D'ye mind the muck and stinkin' poverty fae which Ah
                                                        led ye?

TARTUFFE: Mind it? Sir, ye were mair than generous.
              But affairs o' state are a loat bigger than us!
              An duty demands Ah sacrifice ma personal feelin's
              — Ah tell you, withoot a qualm, nae double dealin's,
              Ah'd name names. Ma Mither Hirsel', if Ah suspect it
              She was now or had ever been infectit
              Wi' the vile contagion o' insurrection —
              Well, ma duty would be tae refuse her protection.

EILMIRE: Hypocrite!

ORGON: An awfy tricky tongue on him! The felly
              Jist turns whit folk haud sacred inty his moral umb'relly . . .

CLÉANTE: Fair enough! But is this zealous loyalty you talk about
              And are (excuse me) so cock-of-the-walk about —
              Is indeed this Pure and Perfect Thing
              Where did it hide itself as you were propositioning
              — To put it *very* mildly — this man's wife?
              I've never heard such fatuous hypocrisy in all my life.
              To denounce him somehow did not occur
              Until he caught you with her
              And, of course, was forced to send you away.
              Now he *had* given you all his property, but I don't say
              You should have let this seduce you from your duty.
              Yet why oh why — et tu Brute, isn't it a beauty? —
              Did your dexterous right hand take and take and take
              While the sinister other stabbed him in the back, and
                                                         no mistake!

TARTUFFE: Officer, this damnable racket is getting on ma nerves.
              We've a guilty man here, gie him whit he deserves.

OFFICER: You're absolutely right, Sir, the sooner we get on wi' it,
              The sooner we'll be ower and done wi' it.
              Mister Tartuffe: I arrest you in the name of the law.
              Your cell's a' swept oot an' ready for you an a' . . .

TARTUFFE: Who, me?

OFFICER: Aye you.

TARTUFFE: Why? Tae the jile . . .?

OFFICER: I don't owe you any explanations, sir, but while
              I don't *need* to tell you nuthin', a' right, I will.
              Mr. Prince hates those who would do justice ill.
              Mr. Prince's most hated enemy is fraud.
              Mr. Prince's eyes, sir, like the Eyes of God,
              Can see inty the depths of the human heart.
              Mr. Prince is proof against the con-man's art.

OFFICER: cont.	Not wan to fall for any cock and bull,
	Nor tae let nae silvertongued pattermerchant pull the wool.

OFFICER: cont.

Not wan to fall for any cock and bull,
Nor tae let nae silvertongued pattermerchant pull the wool.
He's a reasonable man, and wan no' lightly swayed.
His judgements are sound, and balanced, and weighed.
Men o' worth bask in his everlasting favour,
But forgive an act o' treachery? No sir, never!
So: this man convince him? It couldny happen.
— Be up a loat earlier, son, to catch him nappin' —
Seen right through him from the start!
Hoo black, and vile, and twisted, wis his heart.
Wance alertit, Intelligence exposed him as a latterday
Notorious known criminal who, under anither identity,
(Investigations revealed) was guilty of profanity,
Indency, gross moral turpitude and high treason.
Well Mr. Prince had a' ready been gonny punish him — if
                                          fur nae ither reason
Than fur his disloyalty in tryin' tae dae you herm,
An' noo thae ither crimes, a list's long as yir erm!
So I'm here under strict instructions tae let the evil-doer
Go a' the wey wi' his villainy — sort o' 'a-jong provocatoo-er'
As the French cry it — and shair enough
Did he no condemn his-sel' oot o' his ain mooth? No hauf!
So: I'm ordert a' threat o' eviction be removed fae yir heads,
I've tae take this "Deed o' Gift" rip it inty shreds.

(HE DOES SO)

Just men who love the Government needny fear the Law.
Is a contract worth the paper that it's written oan?
                                          Nut at a'!
Thank God Good Government's Sovereign Power can aye
                                          arrange it
That if a law isny servin' Justice, well . . . .they can change it.
Therefore if Orgon was Too Good, and got gulled
By This Wan — the contract is annulled.
Mr. Prince is happy to pardon your . . . wee indiscretion
Wi' the boax of papers — if you've learned yir lesson!
Well, whit's a wee paccadillo compared to the loyalty
You showed him in former times, your defence of royalty
In the face of the forces of lawlessness?
The Monarchy's mibbe All Powerful, but nevertheless
Its memory for a Good Deed is much longer
Than it is for wee mistakes! The Good is stronger!

DORINE: Good God Almighty!

PERNELLE: We can breathe again . . .

ELMIRE: It's over . . .

MARIANNE: Never thought I'd see the day when —

(MARIANNE & VALÈRE KISS)

ORGON: Ya vile an' vicious traitor —

CLÉANTE: Don't descend to his level!
Let Heaven be the one to punish the devil.
Remorse will have to come from him and him alone
When he looks into his blackheart and sees his own
Vileness, owns up to it in genuine repentance.
Then our lenient Prince may modify his sentence.
Orgon, go to Mr. Prince and throw yourself at his feet,
Thank God and him it's clemency and not revenge that's
                                                    sweet.

ORGON: You are right, sir. As ye were a' alang.
Ah'll tell Mr. Prince an a' ma faimily: Ah wis wrang.
But, this duty done, there'll be happier still!
Valère and Marianne wad mairry? Well, they will!
And may they never forget the lesson Ah hae learnt the day.

DORINE: We'll be happy ever eftir. And the band will play.

CURTAIN